119TH OPEN CHAMPIONSHIP
Card of the Old Course

Hole	Par	Yards	Hole	Par	Yards
1	4	370	10	4	342
2	4	411	11	3	172
3	4	371	12	4	316
4	4	463	13	4	425
5	5	564	14	5	567
6	4	416	15	4	413
7	4	372	16	4	382
8	3	178	17	4	461
9	4	356	18	4	354
Out	36	3,501	In	36	3,432
			Total	72	6,933

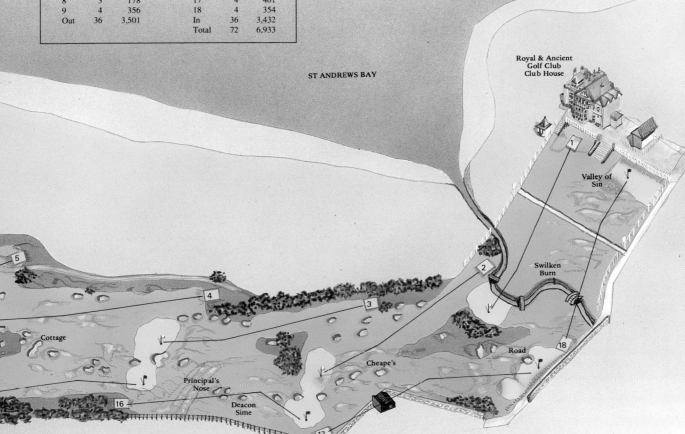

ST ANDREWS BAY

Royal & Ancient
Golf Club
Club House

Valley of
Sin

Swilken
Burn

Cottage

Cheape's

Road

Principal's
Nose

Deacon
Sime

16

17

THE OPEN CHAMPIONSHIP 1990

WRITERS

JOHN HOPKINS
RAYMOND JACOBS
RENTON LAIDLAW
MICHAEL McDONNELL
ALISTER NICOL
MARINO PARASCENZO
MICHAEL WILLIAMS

PHOTOGRAPHERS

LAWRENCE LEVY
BRIAN MORGAN

EDITOR

BEV NORWOOD

AUTHORISED BY THE
CHAMPIONSHIP COMMITTEE
OF THE ROYAL AND ANCIENT
GOLF CLUB OF ST. ANDREWS

TRANSWORLD PUBLISHERS LTD
61-63 Uxbridge Road, London W5 5SA

TRANSWORLD PUBLISHERS (AUSTRALIA) PTY LTD
15-23 Helles Avenue, Moorebank, NSW 2170

TRANSWORLD PUBLISHERS (NZ) LTD
Cnr Moselle and Waipareira Aves,
Henderson, Auckland

Published 1990 by Partridge Press
a division of Transworld Publishers Ltd
Copyright © 1990 The Championship Committee Merchandising
Limited

Statistics of 119th Open Championship produced on a
Unisys Computer System.

All photographs courtesy of Lawrence Levy/Yours in Sport
except pp 31, 70 & 88 courtesy of Matthew Harris

A CIP catalogue record for this book is available
from the British Library

Phototypeset by Falcon Graphic Art Ltd
Printed in Great Britain
by Richard Clay

CONTENTS

Evening descends on the second round of the 119th Open Championship.

THE CHAMPIONSHIP COMMITTEE

CHAIRMAN

G. M. SIMMERS, OBE

DEPUTY CHAIRMAN

R. D. MUCKART JR.

COMMITTEE

H. M. CAMPBELL
A. R. COLE-HAMILTON
J. C. DAWSON
R. FOSTER
P. W. J. GREENHOUGH
D. I. PEPPER
P. G. SHILLINGTON
J. K. TATE
P. M. G. UNSWORTH
W. J. UZIELLI

BUSINESS MEMBER

N. J. CRICHTON

ADDITIONAL MEMBER

D. REA O'KELLY
COUNCIL OF NATIONAL GOLF UNIONS

SECRETARY

M. F. BONALLACK, OBE

DEPUTY SECRETARY

W. G. WILSON

CHAMPIONSHIP SECRETARY

D. HILL

ASSISTANT SECRETARY (CHAMPIONSHIPS)

D. R. WEIR

INTRODUCTION

BY G.M. SIMMERS
Chairman of Championship Committee
Royal and Ancient Golf Club of St Andrews

An Open Championship at St Andrews, the traditional home of golf, is always a special occasion and the 119th Open was no exception. Nearly 210,000 spectators, a record for the event, enjoyed marvellous weather and some fantastic golf.

The historic links were in excellent condition and, without a testing wind on any of the four days, the scores were low, with the cut after two rounds coming at a new low of one under par.

My congratulations to Nick Faldo, who always looked the player the others had to beat and whose 270 aggregate was second only to Tom Watson's 268 record in the history of the Open. A special tribute also to all the competitors, who once again played with their usual high standard of sportsmanship.

The Championship Committee of the Royal and Ancient Golf Club is pleased to present this official annual, which I hope will bring back memories to all those who attended the Championship, either as a spectator, television viewer, or as one of the literally thousands of volunteers who assisted us so well throughout the week.

I would like to thank our contributors, all well respected in the world of golf, for providing this lasting record of the 1990 Championship.

G.M. Simmers, OBE

Nick Faldo's 270 aggregate was the best ever for an Open Championship at St Andrews.

FOREWORD

BY NICK FALDO

This was something quite special – to have won the Open Championship on a week such as this, with the atmosphere of this fabulous town. It is every golfer's dream to win at St Andrews.

When I first started playing, I would be on the putting green and would say, 'This is to win the Open' . . . and I would always be thinking of St Andrews.

This is the ultimate place to win, the Home of Golf. You don't have to be a history buff to appreciate that nearly every great golfer before you has walked over that same Swilken Bridge.

The key for the whole week was my iron play. I missed only two greens unintentionally, and I played the seventeenth defensively, which was the right thing to do. You are always worried about the seventeenth, even before you arrive. My putting also was fabulous all week.

I won with the support of a lot of people, but especially my parents and my wife, Gill; my coach, David Leadbetter, and my caddie, Fanny Sunneson. I wish that George Blumberg and Gerald Micklem, two great friends, could have lived to see this, but I believe they must have been looking down and enjoying my victory.

Nick Faldo

119TH OPEN CHAMPIONSHIP

* Denotes amateurs

NAME	SCORES				TOTAL	MONEY
Nick Faldo, England	67	65	67	71	270	£85,000
Mark McNulty, Zimbabwe	74	68	68	65	275	60,000
Payne Stewart, USA	68	68	68	71	275	60,000
Jodie Mudd, USA	72	66	72	66	276	40,000
Ian Woosnam, Wales	68	69	70	69	276	40,000
Greg Norman, Australia	66	66	76	69	277	28,500
Ian Baker-Finch, Australia	68	72	64	73	277	28,500
David Graham, Australia	72	71	70	66	279	22,000
Steve Pate, USA	70	68	72	69	279	22,000
Donnie Hammond, USA	70	71	68	70	279	22,000
Corey Pavin, USA	71	69	68	71	279	22,000
Vijay Singh, Fiji	70	69	72	69	280	16,375
Robert Gamez, USA	70	72	67	71	280	16,375
Tim Simpson, USA	70	69	69	72	280	16,375
Paul Broadhurst, England	74	69	63	74	280	16,375
Mark Roe, England	71	70	72	68	281	11,150
Steve Jones, USA	72	67	72	70	281	11,150
Jose Maria Olazabal, Spain	71	67	71	72	281	11,150
Sandy Lyle, Scotland	72	70	67	72	281	11,150
Peter Jacobsen, USA	68	70	70	73	281	11,150
Frank Nobilo, New Zealand	72	67	68	74	281	11,150
Eamonn Darcy, Ireland	71	71	72	68	282	7,933
James Spence, England	72	65	73	72	282	7,933
Craig Parry, Australia	68	68	69	77	282	7,933
Lee Trevino, USA	69	70	73	71	283	6,383
Jeff Sluman, USA	72	70	70	71	283	6,383
Christy O'Connor, Jr., Ireland	68	72	71	72	283	6,383
Fred Couples, USA	71	70	70	72	283	6,383
Jose Rivero, Spain	70	70	70	73	283	6,383
Nick Price, Zimbabwe	70	67	71	75	283	6,383
Ronan Rafferty, N. Ireland	70	71	73	70	284	5,125
Larry Mize, USA	71	72	70	71	284	5,125
Mark James, England	73	69	70	72	284	5,125
Mark McCumber, USA	69	74	69	72	284	5,125
Greg Powers, USA	74	69	69	72	284	5,125
Ben Crenshaw, USA	74	69	68	73	284	5,125
Bryan Norton, USA	71	72	68	73	284	5,125
Vicente Fernandez, Argentina	72	67	69	76	284	5,125
Naomichi Ozaki, Japan	71	71	74	69	285	4,217
Andy North, USA	71	71	72	71	285	4,217
Raymond Floyd, USA	72	71	71	71	285	4,217
Don Pooley, USA	70	73	71	71	285	4,217
Sam Torrance, Scotland	68	70	75	72	285	4,217
Derrick Cooper, England	72	71	69	73	285	4,217
Scott Simpson, USA	73	70	69	73	285	4,217
Mike Reid, USA	70	67	73	75	285	4,217
Mike Hulbert, USA	70	70	70	75	285	4,217
Bernhard Langer, Germany	74	69	75	68	286	3,720
Colin Montgomerie, Scotland	72	69	74	71	286	3,720
Mark O'Meara, USA	70	69	73	74	286	3,720
Peter Fowler, Australia	73	68	71	74	286	3,720
Paul Azinger, USA	73	68	68	77	286	3,720

Hale Irwin, USA	72	68	75	72	287	3,475
John Bland, South Africa	71	72	72	72	287	3,475
Eduardo Romero, Argentina	69	71	74	73	287	3,475
Michael Allen, USA	66	75	73	73	287	3,475
Jim Rutledge, USA	71	69	76	72	288	3,225
Michael Clayton, Australia	72	71	72	73	288	3,225
Blaine McCallister, USA	71	68	75	74	288	3,225
Danny Mijovic, Canada	69	74	71	74	288	3,225
David Ray, England	71	69	73	75	288	3,225
Anders Sorensen, Denmark	70	68	71	79	288	3,225
Jack Nicklaus, USA	71	70	77	71	289	2,950
Peter Baker, England	73	68	75	73	289	2,950
Roger Chapman, England	72	70	74	73	289	2,950
Martin Poxon, England	68	72	74	75	289	2,950
David Canipe, USA	72	70	69	78	289	2,950
David Feherty, N. Ireland	74	69	71	76	290	2,775
Jorge Berendt, Argentina	75	66	72	77	290	2,775
Armando Saavedra, Argentina	72	69	75	75	291	2,700
Malcolm Mackenzie, England	70	71	76	75	292	2,700
Jose Maria Canizares, Spain	72	70	78	76	296	2,700

NON QUALIFIERS AFTER 36 HOLES
(All professionals receive £500)

Arnold Palmer, USA	73	71	144
Tom Kite, USA	71	73	144
Rick Hartman, USA	73	71	144
Wayne Westner, South Africa	72	72	144
Mike Harwood, Australia	72	72	144
John Morgan, England	74	70	144
Jeff Woodland, Australia	73	71	144
Greg Turner, New Zealand	69	75	144
Brian Barnes, Scotland	73	71	144
Juan Quiros, Spain	73	71	144
Curtis Strange, USA	74	71	145
Tom Watson, USA	72	73	145
Lanny Wadkins, USA	71	74	145
Bob Estes, USA	73	72	145
Bill Glasson, USA	72	73	145
David Frost, South Africa	72	73	145
Steve Elkington, Australia	74	71	145
Gary Player, South Africa	72	73	145
Chris Moody, England	71	74	145
Stephen Bennett, England	74	71	145
Patrick Hall, England	74	71	145
Paul Mayo, Wales	73	72	145
* Tony Nash, England	73	72	145
Andrew Oldcorn, England	74	71	145
Seve Ballesteros, Spain	71	74	145
Howard Clark, England	73	72	145
Andrew Hare, England	73	72	145
Mikael Krantz, Sweden	72	73	145
David Williams, England	74	71	145

Mark Calcavecchia, USA	71	75	146
Bob Tway, USA	73	73	146
Kenny Knox, USA	74	72	146
Paul Curry, England	72	74	146
Ross Drummond, Scotland	75	71	146
Wayne Player, South Africa	76	70	146
Miguel Martin, Spain	74	72	146
Peter Hedblom, Sweden	75	71	146
John Huston, USA	77	70	147
Tom Weiskopf, USA	73	74	147
Tommy Armour III, USA	74	73	147
Scott Hoch, USA	71	76	147
Wayne Grady, Australia	73	74	147
Jose Gervas, Spain	78	69	147
Des Smyth, Ireland	73	74	147
Peter Senior, Australia	72	75	147
Masashi Ozaki, Japan	72	75	147
Denis Durnian, England	73	74	147
Philip Harrison, England	72	75	147
Gordon Brand, Jr., Scotland	77	70	147
Peter Mitchell, England	72	75	147
Ken Green, USA	73	75	148
Davis Love III, USA	73	75	148
Richard Boxall, England	78	70	148
Brett Ogle, Australia	78	70	148
Jeff Hawkes, South Africa	75	73	148
Kenneth Trimble, Australia	75	73	148
David A. Russell, England	75	73	148
David Jones, N. Ireland	74	74	148
Brian Jones, Australia	72	76	148
Stewart Ginn, Australia	73	75	148
Paul Archbold, Australia	78	70	148

* Chris Patton, USA	74	75	149
Gavin Levenson, South Africa	75	74	149
Ossie Moore, Australia	74	75	149
* Yasunobu Kuramoto, Japan	77	72	149
Philip Walton, Ireland	74	75	149
Mark Mouland, Wales	76	73	149
Jose Davila, Spain	74	75	149
Yutaka Hagawa, Japan	78	71	149
Keith Waters, England	76	74	150
Andrew Murray, England	74	76	150
Russell Weir, Scotland	77	73	150
Chip Beck, USA	76	75	151
Isao Aoki, Japan	73	78	151
Bob Charles, New Zealand	76	75	151
Paul Hoad, England	75	76	151
Joe Higgins, England	78	73	151
Paul Way, England	75	77	152
Graham Farr, England	82	70	152
* Rolf Muntz, Jr., Netherlands	78	74	152
Craig Stadler, USA	82	71	153
Rodger Davis, Australia	82	71	153
Paul Lyons, England	77	76	153
Ricardo Gonzalez, Argentina	75	78	153

Perhaps the most dramatic scene in golf is the seventy-second hole of the Open Championship.

ROUND THE OLD COURSE

No. 1 370 YARDS, PAR 4

Deserves the distinction of having been described as 'the widest fairway in Christendom'. Essentially a second-shot hole, where the approach over the Swilcan Burn must be precisely clubbed to finish near the flagstick, usually positioned just the far side of the hazard.

No. 2 411 YARDS, PAR 4

Given less than its due. Only the longest hitter will reach Cheape's Bunker on the left, but anyway the best line from which to attack the hole, usually on the top left of the green, is from the right. To underclub from either angle is to leave the player with a taxingly difficult pitch or first putt.

No. 3 371 YARDS, PAR 4

Ideally, the drive should be to the right where, however, a succession of pot bunkers and bushes lie in wait for the shot too greedy for space. The object, as at the previous hole, is to coax the ball near to a flagstick set at the foot of an abrupt slope.

No. 4 463 YARDS, PAR 4

The tee shot is either right, down the 'drain-pipe' between a rough bank and bunkers, or across the raised ground to the left. The second is, as ever, hard to judge, but there is ample room to the right and since the arrival of the yardage chart the hump short of the green has become less troublesome.

No. 5 564 YARDS, PAR 5

About 250 yards from the tee, on the edge of the right rough, lie a cluster of seven bunkers. In the face of a hill short of the green are two more bunkers, beyond which there is a deep gully. The initial line is more to the left, after which shots should be aimed directly at the flagstick.

No. 6 416 YARDS, PAR 4

The fairway is all but hidden from the tee by a bank of whins and the drive must avoid bunkers on both sides of the fairway. In front of the green a sharp rise hides a dip in the ground. First be accurate, then do not be short.

No. 7 372 YARDS, PAR 4

The start of the famous Loop of six holes where a score can be hugely improved or fatally compromised. The bold tee-shot will skirt the mass of whins to the right and the approach, over Cockle Bunker, must be firm enough to scale the green's steep frontal slope.

No. 8 178 YARDS, PAR 3

The first of the course's only two short holes. Over broken ground there is a little hill inset with a quite deep bunker, behind which the hole is customarily cut. The straightest line of attack is the best.

No. 9 356 YARDS, PAR 4

Given the right conditions, every player will hope for a birdie. To avoid whins and bunkers and drive close to the green should not be difficult; the second shot is not easy to judge, for the green is not built up or closely guarded, merely an extension of the flat fairway and thus optically elusive.

No. 10 342 YARDS, PAR 4

As with the previous hole, eminently driveable downwind. There is room to spare on the right, away from whins and a cunningly placed bunker almost in the fairway's centre. A steep little crest protects the green, which slopes back, and three putts here are commonplace.

No. 11 172 YARDS, PAR 3

Among the most famous and copied holes in the world. The green, precipitously sloping from back to front, is much wider than it is deep. Its twin sentries are Hill and Strath Bunkers, the latter lying between the player and the tightest pin position.

No. 12 316 YARDS, PAR 4

A nest of bunkers, concealed from the tee, creates a minefield. Take the right or left line, but from wherever the pitch to a narrow shelf of green, with quite steep slopes front and rear, is seldom less than precarious.

No. 13 425 YARDS, PAR 4

From the tee the appropriately named Coffin Bunker and Walkinshaw's, all to the left, must first be avoided. The crumpled ground short of the green may divert the ball into the Lion's Mouth or Hole o'Cross Bunkers; perversely, the green itself slopes sharply away from the player.

No. 14 567 YARDS, PAR 5

On the right the boundary wall, to the left the four Beardies Bunkers, beyond the sanctuary of the Elysian Fields. The mass of Hell Bunker and a series of smaller traps beyond must be negotiated to a raised green with more than enough borrow to demand concentration.

No. 15 413 YARDS, PAR 4

The preferred line from the tee is on the church spire between two large mounds. The second shot is deceptive, being longer than it seems. The best approach is slightly to the left and boldness, rather than caution, is more likely to be rewarded.

No. 16 382 YARDS, PAR 4

The 'amateur' line is between the Principal's Nose Bunkers and the out-of-bounds fence. The wiser alternative is to hold left and play the approach over Wig Bunker to the hole beyond an abrupt upslope.

No. 17 461 YARDS, PAR 4

The sting in the tail to end them all, as much a psychological as a physical examination. Drive over the reproduction of the old coal sheds as boldly to the right as possible to gain position for the second shot. Few will attack the hole; the Road Bunker and the road itself behind the raised green are golf's most notorious Scylla and Charybdis.

No. 18 354 YARDS, PAR 4

Sharing its fairway with the first hole, no terror from the tee and the green has frequently been driven. The hazards to avoid are the road on the right and the Valley of Sin, the deep depression guarding the flagstick. On the green, though, nothing is quite what it seems.

THE 'REAL' ST ANDREWS

BY RAYMOND JACOBS

Although it may appear treasonable even to suggest it, St Andrews is far from being its traditional best during the Open Championship. There is no help for it. The ghosts of its history, the unique atmosphere of the place, and its familiar setting are inevitably submerged beneath the paraphernalia of the event. The grandstands, the tentage and the hum and bustle generate their own excitement and the anticipation of great things to come. You could almost wish for the players that they could have the Old Course to themselves, as it is on a fine May morning or a golden September afternoon, when 'every prospect pleases' and the game itself is all that matters. That is the real St Andrews.

The real St Andrews? Well, what other course starts and finishes in the middle of a place instead of in some wide-open space? To many that vast expansive fairway, shared by the first and eighteenth holes, has a disconcerting habit of shrinking in the most penal manner. Hit the opening and closing drives as far left as you dare, but those white fences on the right twice threaten. Who, furthermore, has not drowned his second shot to the first hole in the Swilcan Burn or seen his approach to the eighteenth hole fall into the Valley of Sin? Who has not also trembled slightly under the gaze of the curious spectators who hang over the fence behind the Tom Morris green to take in the action?

Thousands will have done the same from their pre-fabricated vantage points as the challengers for the title of Champion Golfer for the Year play out the last act. Of course, some of them may, within hours afterwards, be putting their decidedly humbler games to a similar test, following in the footsteps of the contemporary masters of the game, glowing if they can match the figure of one of their heroes at this hole or that. For, distinguished in this way from almost every other participant sport, the most modestly handicapped amateur can enter the same arena as the mightiest of all professionals.

Yet, despite appearances, both city and links survive the invasion with that sense of detachment that comes from knowing with confidence that history remains firmly on their side. No other golfing site on earth – however spectacular or groomed or equipped, however considered or preposterous the claims made for its character may be – carries the same appeal. Indeed, St Andrews has been said to be not so much a place for golf as a state of mind. It is to golfers what Florence is to artists and Paris to lovers. Like the mediaeval traveller who had not seen Avignon in Papal times, the golfer who has not seen St Andrews has seen nothing. It is the world's least exclusive shrine.

Both the city and the university of St Andrews have had an inextricable association with the establishment and evolution of a game which took its improbable root in the East Neuk of Fife, before it spread to every part of the world, civilized and otherwise. Briefly, the city received its charter in the 1100s; the university, founded in 1410, is the oldest in Britain, except for some of the colleges at Oxford and Cambridge; and the first written record of golf at St Andrews dates from 1457, the implication being that the game was well established by that date. But bad times were just around the corner.

Following its foundation as a place of pilgrimage to the bones of the saint who gave his name to the city, St Andrews became Scotland's ecclesiastical centre and a busy port. Brutal and destructive conflicts, between the Protestants and Roman Catholics, eventually propelled St Andrews into an alarming decline. By the late eighteenth century the population had shrunk from 15,000 to 2,000 and, as was written

The ancient Swilken Bridge, with the Royal and Ancient Clubhouse in the distance.

at the time, 'grass grew in the streets.' The city's motto, *Dum Spiro, Spero* (While I breathe, I hope), was never more apt in defining its successful recovery. It was, just as appropriately, readily transferable as a philosophy for golf.

Perhaps the continuing need to develop the healthy mind in the healthy body, helped both golf and the university survive. Both continued to dominate the city's life. The legacy of the various upheavals, however, had the effect of creating a tourist attraction which was to confer on St Andrews the celebrated verdict that 'there is no place in Scotland over which the genius of antiquity lingers so impressively.' Precisely the same description could be applied to the Old Course. Not everyone has been initially convinced, not excluding Bobby Jones, who, as all the world knows, tore up his card when his first acquaintance turned out to be less than unforgettable. But, what began for Jones as a gnawing aversion later became an abiding respect.

Some say God made the course by way of a practice shot before He addressed himself to the serious business of the Creation. Others insist that instead of resting on the seventh day He devised the links simply as a means of keeping His hand in. Others still maintain that He allowed this unique stretch of coastline to emerge in nothing less than a fit of absent-mindedness. Actually, what happened was that this terrain surfaced as the sea withdrew – 'a perfect example of an original layout of nature, interpreted and completed by beast and man,' as Sir Guy Campbell, the golf historian, so evocatively put it.

The next stage in the process of evolution was that the sandy wastes dried out into hollows, ridges, dunes and knolls, creating the unique character of the British seaside course. Bird droppings helped to fertilize the seeds blown from the land and rabbits were attracted by the grasses, making runs among the heather, whins and broom, which later still were widened by animals of prey and, lastly, man, the hunter. As late as the mid-nineteenth century the Old Course's narrow strip of ground allowed only for eleven and then nine single greens – the same hole had to be played out and back, hence the origin of the eighteen-hole course.

This triumph of the evolution of nature over the mechanical digger, this exercise in judgement and blind faith over the inflexible calculations of the yardage chart has never ceased to challenge the mental processes of the great and the good, yet has proved to be a sporting examination to the games of lesser breeds. Those crumpled fairways, hidden hazards, enormous double greens, and, perhaps most baffling of all to the modern professional, the almost complete absence of target definition, have made the Old Course a museum piece which could be placed in a gallery of modern golfing art.

Later, the greens were extended laterally, producing the seven huge double surfaces for which the Old Course is famous – or notorious, depending on the player's accuracy with his second shots and the weight and line of his putts. It is often said that Arnold Palmer did not win the first Open he entered thirty years ago because he persistently saw borrows that did not exist on the holing-out putts, those from ten feet and less. The local rule of thumb is that from such distances it is almost always prudent to aim for inside the hole, instead of allowing for some angular lie of the land which turns out to be nothing more than an optical illusion.

Human nature being its perverse self, of course, not every player readily learns how to stop worrying and love the Old Course for those features which, by some modern architectural philosophies, are as dotty as some aged retainer who has passed well beyond his shelf life. How, for instance, can there be any justification for the obvious unfairness bestowed on awkward lies of stances to balls only feet apart? The seventeenth, the treacherous seventeenth, the notorious Road Hole, annually replenishes the stock of natural disasters, but the first and eighteenth, whose shared expanse of fairway must be the broadest in golfing Christendom, caused fifteen players in the 1978 Open Championship to take six or more.

Fairness is not what the Old Course is about, although it is remarkable how well the most modestly equipped golfers score over it, particularly at first acquaintance, but also when they play it at rare intervals. Their ignorance can be bliss. There were sharp intakes of breath when Curtis Strange,

playing in the Dunhill Cup of 1987, set a record of 62, ten under par. This was seen as taking something of a liberty and, indeed, brought back memories of 1964, when Tony Lema, after a minimum of practice, won the Open Championship at his first attempt. The Championship Committee of that year actually agonized whether the Old Course had become too easy, past its best as a proper examination of the contemporary professional golfer.

Mercifully, they had the sense to reach the conclusion that the criterion was who won, not by how many or with what total. This decision was more than amply supported by the next four champions at St Andrews – Jack Nicklaus, in 1970 and 1978, Severiano Ballesteros in 1984, and Nick Faldo this year. It is a curious anomaly that, whereas in other sports the breaking of records is regarded as evidence of improved preparation, technique or equipment, a resistance to lower scores in golf remains widespread and persistent. After all, the incalculable factors of the weather, the lie and the bounce and roll of the ball will not suddenly release a swarm of scores in the 50s as if it were the first sub-four-minute mile, which removed a barrier more psychological than physical.

It is surely possible – essential now in these days when professional golf has outgrown the naivety which thought of it as being 'merely a game', beyond just an opportunity for a gilded few to earn vast sums and for lesser mortals also to prosper, to the position of being public entertainers – to take the game seriously without being crushingly solemn about it. Tom Watson once expressed a plaintive *cri de coeur*, remarking on the structured way in which courses for the US Open are prepared and set up: 'Why don't they stop changing courses just for the sake of making them more difficult and let us get on with scoring the best we can?' Which brings us back to the question of the Old Course as an adequate examination for the games of the modern professional.

To alter any of it would be unthinkable; one might as well propose wiping that enigmatic smile from the Mona Lisa. Take out a bunker? Let the rough grow in here? Root out a line of whin bushes there? Introduce a water hazard somewhere? What sacrilegious thoughts. By all means alter other courses if that is thought to be necessary, but the Old Course has an astonishing knack for resisting advances of technique and equipment by being as quizzical as the expression on that famous portrait itself. It remains as a portrait which is ancient, yet capable of fitting comfortably into the frame of modern golf. In its changelessness rests its timelessness.

Jack Nicklaus has now played the final day in twenty-eight Open Championships.

NICKLAUS AND ST ANDREWS

BY MICHAEL McDONNELL

Perhaps the greatest favour Jack Nicklaus has accorded history is that he leaves no obvious gaps in his phenomenal career; no niggling omissions that might make his record subject to argument and debate.

It is a thoroughness that has not only ensured all the major titles were won more than once but that they were captured invariably on the great venues of the sport, as if to underline the stature of the man and his achievements.

Inevitably, therefore, the Golfer of the Century presented himself at the Home of Golf to leave his own indelible mark upon the place and add to its great history by the drama of his deeds.

His name will forever be linked with the Old Course, for he captured the Open twice upon it. But just as importantly he captured the hearts and esteem of the townsfolk. Moreover, he received an honorary Doctorate of Law from the University of St Andrews, and while all of it is clear evidence of an acknowledgement and respect by the local folk for the greatest golfer of his time, there is more to it; as though they know he shares with them a regard for the Old Course that makes him essentially a St Andrean.

It may not, of course, be love for the Old Course that he exudes. In fact, the late Gerald Micklem, a most perceptive observer of golf and golfers as well as being a noted authority on the Old Course, had his own theory about the relationship between Jack Nicklaus and St Andrews.

He said: 'I think Jack is tremendously inspired by the Old Course, but whether he likes it is another matter. He has a great capacity to cope better than most with whatever he finds.'

What Nicklaus found when he first beheld the Old Course in the 1964 Open was living testimony to his own philosophy that golf was never meant to be a fair game. The Old Course, as the origin of the species, defined that original arbitrary aspect of a pursuit which tests the man as much as his skill.

More than this, it defined what golf was meant to be; or rather, the precise nature of the challenge that put it far beyond a simple question of skill but into an area of human endeavour where random twists of fortune – good and bad – were essential and had to be accepted with equanimity.

He was met that year by galeforce conditions the likes of which he had never witnessed before or since, as he said at the 1990 Open. He had been the random victim of the starting sheet and was thus obliged to take on the Old Course in the worst of weather on the first day to produce a 76 and, after two rounds, found himself nine strokes behind Tony Lema's leading score.

As conditions improved, so did Jack's golf, but if he held any hopes that a third round 66 might improve his chances, he was to be mistaken because he had managed only to reduce the gap between them to seven strokes after his fellow countryman scored 68 on his way to what was to be the glittering high point of an all-too-brief career. Within two years, Lema had been killed in a plane crash.

What appealed to Nicklaus about the Old Course was that it insisted a player – or in Lema's case, his caddie – did his homework; that he knew the safe routes and target areas and stuck rigidly to the game plan.

It is a matter of historical fact that nobody ever prepared better than Jack Nicklaus for a championship. What separated him from his rivals was his high degree of research and study of a course in fine detail, as well as his measurement of precise yardages which left nothing to chance or doubt.

Nicklaus' 77 in the third round kept him off the leaderboard.

In a sense, therefore, Nicklaus and the Old Course have always been worthy opponents and what success he has earned from it over the years has been a direct result of the respect and reverence he has displayed, because such attitudes also dictated the correct strategy. At St Andrews, he has always been the epitome of patience and restraint.

Except just once, of course. And that incident is now part of golf lore. The background to the staggering stroke that won him the 1970 Open is essential because it demonstrated the importance of St Andrews to him at a crucial period of his life.

He had been the all-conquering hero, apart from minor hiccups, since winning the 1962 US Open within months of turning professional. Thereafter he had scooped a reasonable and frequent ration of major titles on a yearly basis and by 1966 had completed the Grand Slam of all four major championships, though not in the same year.

Then suddenly it all stopped. From the moment he won the 1967 US Open at Baltusrol, he could not seem to take a firm grasp of another major. In fact the next twelve majors were to pass him by and so nearly did the Open at St Andrews, but for that short downhill putt which Doug Sanders missed on the last green to become outright champion.

So it was the next day that they came to the play-off and in particular to the last hole of that encounter when Nicklaus stood on the tee and pondered whether to go for the green, 354 yards away. The risks were enormous because the slightest error would send the ball over the fence to the right and out of bounds and almost certainly give Sanders the title.

What had plagued Nicklaus in the previous twelve majors had been a crisis of confidence. In truth, his old intimidating, self-assured manner, which could wither a damn-fool questioner at a glance, had all but vanished. What we saw at St Andrews that year was a gentler man who perhaps had been mellowed by misfortune and who had come to accept he wasn't superman and that success was never guaranteed.

But in that moment he needed to find some of that old self-belief and the conviction that brings a sure hand to the task. The crowds which thronged the last hole soon received the message for which they had waited. He removed his sweater and reached for the driver.

When launched, the ball sped unerringly towards its target at a furious pace. In fact, it had been too well struck because it raced to the back of the green, from where Nicklaus chipped down, then holed an 8-footer to win a championship he was convinced had passed him by.

He jumped joyfully into the air and hurled his putter heavenwards. It was the first time the rest of the human race had ever seen 'superman' display any emotion. In fact, both he and the ill-fated Sanders had to dodge the putter as it came back to earth. Even so, Jack was a champion again.

Something else had happened too. He had become a hero. It will stand as the moment the Scottish crowds, who had always respected his golf, suddenly grew to love the man. And it has not changed these twenty years on. They remember – can they ever forget? – how he held the trophy in his hands that day, and blinking back the tears, said: 'I would like a second or two to savour this moment.' Then both he and the thousands around him fell silent.

Of course, the win had been desperately needed to heave his championship career out of the doldrums, but that it should happen at the Home of Golf seemed to hold the seal of higher approval, as well as suggesting this man could never be written off.

And yet eight years later he came back to St Andrews and was in apparent decline again, only this time his critics and some supporters shared the belief that this really was the end of the Nicklaus era. He was now thirty-eight and had endured two fruitless championship seasons and seen ten successive majors slip by (though not without a fight as he demonstrated with his 1977 Turnberry showdown against Tom Watson).

In any case in 1978 at St Andrews, he seemed to be cast in a supporting role on the final day of the championship as Tom Watson battled with Peter Oosterhuis a stroke ahead of him, with a certain young hopeful named Nick Faldo just a stroke behind him (no doubt wondering perhaps what fate

eventually had in store for him).

Yet as soon as Nicklaus looked out of his bedroom window on the morning of that final day and saw that the wind was coming from the west, he knew he had a chance. The others had not played it all week from that direction but he had arrived at St Andrews several days before all of them and played it in practice. He knew which hazards came into play, particularly from the tee on the homeward stretch.

Accordingly, he played with patience and restraint using a three wood from the tee to take the hazards out of play and keep his ball safely on the fairways. Even on the Road Hole, he played dutifully for the front of the green rather than take the risk of racing on to the road behind. It was the perfect ploy, because his wisdom and experience took him past his younger rivals and on to victory by a two-stroke margin.

Thus the Old Course and Jack Nicklaus have been good for each other. They are old acquaintances and curiously enough each brings out the best in the other by revealing strengths and qualities that might otherwise go unnoticed.

While the Scottish fans always made their devotion and esteem obvious to their hero, he also explained how he felt when he accepted his honorary degree in the week of the 1984 Open at St Andrews.

He told the assembled gathering at the Younger Hall: 'I love the style and atmosphere of Scottish golf and the great Scottish linksland courses. I am also in constant awe of the variety and beauty of Scottish terrain.

'But what has always made me love Scotland the most is the people. Nowhere on earth have I been received more warmly, more affectionately or with greater understanding than by the people of this country. I can assure you that the memories of my times here will never fade.'

Nor for those who witnessed his times either. Mr Micklem got it absolutely right when he said: 'I like to think that the winner at St Andrews has been rewarded because he understands its strategic rather than penal qualities.

'I have come to the conclusion that St Andrews remains the ultimate and complete test of a golfer. I do not think you can consider yourself a great golfer unless you play well at St Andrews. Winning at St Andrews sets even the champions apart. There are Opens. And then there are Opens at St Andrews.'

Therein lies the true tribute to the greatness of Jack Nicklaus, the man who triumphed twice upon the ground where the game began.

Greg Norman was blazing with a 66, and seldom has an Open Championship come so quickly to life.

1

A SWIFT START
IN IDEAL CONDITIONS

BY MICHAEL WILLIAMS

There were two winners of the Open Championship this year. The one everybody knew was Nick Faldo. The one a great many did not know was Walter Woods, the head greenkeeper, who, in his own way, made it all possible. For months beforehand there had been dire concern over the condition of the Old Course at St Andrews. As the spiritual home of golf and open not only to the British public but a tidal wave of overseas visitors, the Old Course suffers some 40,000 rounds of golf a year which, one need hardly add, means a great deal of wear and tear. Consequently, it threatened to be a very worn and threadbare course that staged the game's showpiece of the year, the one that everybody, from players to spectators, put before any other.

What made things even worse this year was the abnormally low rainfall, beginning in 1989 and continuing into 1990 with only about one and a half inches of rain before the end of May. In February the Royal and Ancient Golf Club, in conjunction with the St Andrews Links Trust, which has control of all the St Andrews courses, announced their contingency plans. The Old Course would, as usual, be closed throughout the month of March and would also be closed to the public from the beginning of July. Furthermore, in the intervening three months the first starting times each day would be put back to 8 a.m. instead of 6 a.m. and these would now be at intervals of ten minutes rather than eight between each start, all of which meant 20 per cent less play.

There were further savings. The R&A offered to stage the annual Spring Meeting, which draws some 400 members from all parts of the globe, on the New Course instead of on the Old. The same happened to both the St Andrews Links Trophy, now one of the leading amateur events, and the Golf Foundation's Schools Championship.

Even so, there were still St Andreans who were throwing up their hands in horror at the decidedly seedy look the Old Course continued to have, and the local press was not slow to condemn. Through it all Walter Woods remained calm. He was convinced that all would be well, and said so. He knew what he was about, burning off the bad grass of the previous year, replacing it with new fescue, and insisting that by July the Old Course would be in better condition than it had ever been for an Open Championship. Then in late June and early July came the rains.

The condition of the Old Course was quite the best anyone could remember. The Americans, who had been here the previous September for the Dunhill Cup, could not believe it. On top of all that, the championship was blessed with sublime weather. This made for an outstanding week, one of record scores as well as record crowds (nearly 210,000 for the four days), a record entry and record prize money.

There is a very special air about an Open at St Andrews. Nowhere else on earth are the first tee and the eighteenth green so close to the centre of town, but a few minutes' walk from the shops and even less from at least four hotels which, naturally, are in high demand. It is everyone's dream to attend an Open at St Andrews. So much has happened here over the centuries that it has taken books to chronicle it all. More ghosts walk here than anywhere else, for so little has changed. Never a new green, never a new bunker, seldom even a new tee and certainly not one this year.

It is almost exactly the same now as it was when Tom Kidd won in 1873, and J.H. Taylor (1895 and 1900) and James Braid (1905 and 1910) won twice in succession. It is the same as it was when a despairing Bobby Jones tore up his card in the 1921 Open; the same as when Bobby Locke was forgiven for incorrectly replacing his ball before holing his winning putt in 1957; the same as when Tony Lema conquered it at his first glance in 1964; and the same as when Jack Nicklaus hurled his putter to the sky when he beat Doug Sanders in a play-off in 1970.

It was the same, too, when in 1984 a little-known twenty-three-year-old Australian, Ian Baker-Finch, led going into the last round and took 79 as Severiano Ballesteros defeated Tom Watson over the last two holes. It is something with which Baker-Finch has had to live, just as Sanders has always had to live with the short putt he missed to win. In 1990, Baker-Finch had thought about little else over the preceding twelve months, but there were no privileges for what he was so close to doing six years earlier – he had to pre-qualify.

And qualify he did at Scotscraig, one of five courses in use, with rounds of 68 and 65 which, astonishingly, was good enough only for a share of fifth place. Such was the late rush of entries, taking them to a record 1,707, that at the last minute Panmure had to be added to the original list just as South Herts had been for the regional qualifying. The quality of scoring at Scotscraig was by no means exceptional and it gives some idea of how hot the competition is these days. So it remained through the four days of the championship when, once again, Baker-Finch was to play a central role. In his case, history was, to an extent, to repeat itself.

One of the more intriguing side issues in the days leading up to the championship was the announcement of the draw because of the colourful partnerships it threw up. For instance, Nick Faldo, who went into the championship as the favourite, was drawn to play with Scott Hoch, the man he had beaten in a play-off when he won his first Masters in 1989. Then there was Greg Norman, the second favourite, playing with Bob Tway and Robert Gamez, two men who had previously beaten him with miraculous shots, Tway by holing a bunker shot to win the 1986 PGA Championship and Gamez by holing a seven-iron shot earlier this year to rob him of the Bay Hill tournament.

There were memories also for Severiano Ballesteros and Tom Watson, the victor and the vanquished of the 1984 Open as they, too, were drawn together. So too were Ian Woosnam and Curtis Strange, opponents in the crucial last single of the tied 1989 Ryder Cup match as well as in the US Open that year, when Strange won and Woosnam was joint second.

If there was the smell of a 'plant' about all this, the R&A denied it. Michael Bonallack, the secretary, pointed out that there are thirty-two seeded matches, each made up of top players from around the world. Since, according to Bonallack, they are then numbered, the R&A did not realize exactly what they had done until after they had done it.

Spice, nevertheless, had been added. When Thursday morning dawned bright with hardly a breath of wind to break the glass-like sea out in St Andrews Bay, no one needed to be told that the Old Course was there to be taken apart. Twice in three days in the Dunhill Cup of 1987, Rodger Davis, of Australia, had set one new course record with a 63. Forty-eight hours later Strange had beaten it with a 62. Were these to be forerunners of what was to come? Not quite, but not far off it either.

Seldom has any Open come so swiftly to life. At once the big guns came out firing, Norman with a 66 to tie the lead with Michael Allen, of America, and Faldo third with a 67. Right behind came Ian Woosnam, who was the form horse of the moment, having won both the Monte Carlo Open (with a last round of 60) and the Scottish Open (that included a second round of 62) in the two previous weeks. There had been some concern over a niggling back injury in the days leading up to the championship, but a 68 quickly put that to rights.

Woosnam was in quite a pack along with Baker-Finch, another Australian, Craig Parry, Martin Poxon, Christy O'Connor, Jr, Sam Torrance and two Americans in Payne Stewart and Peter Jacobsen. Lee Trevino, now fifty and eighteen years after his second Open Championship victory at Muirfield in 1972, was among five more who also broke 70. The others were Eduardo Romero (Argentina), Greg Turner (New Zealand), Danny Mijovic (Canada), and Mark McCumber (United States).

Altogether thirty players, including the holder, Mark Calcavecchia (71), in a field of 156 broke

Ian Woosnam was not the first, nor the last, to take on the Road Bunker.

the par of 72 while another thirty equalled it. For all that, there were still casualties. None were more spectacular than Craig Stadler, the former American Masters champion, who invariably seems to be a victim of the British climate, balmy though it was this year. He finished, together with Rodger Davis, back marker with an 82, only 34 of which were taken on the inward half. In other words, he took 48 to the turn, running up two sevens, one of them on the sixth green where he five-putted, missing the ball altogether with one attempt.

Greg Norman has so often hung a weight around his neck early on – for instance the 78 he took in the first round of this year's Masters – that it was refreshing to see him imposing himself straightaway and playing with such total command. Something of a breeze picked up in the middle of the day, but not enough to make things really difficult. Norman, always a great favourite in Britain, picked all the greens off one by one and mostly in the right places. There were just a couple of occasions when he had to work rather hard on his second putts but each time he got them in.

A birdie at the first, where he holed from 3 or 4 yards, quickly settled any of Norman's nerves. He made another at the long fifth to be out in 34 but it was not until the inward half that he captured the form that had taken him to the top of the money list in America. More birdies followed at the tenth, twelfth and fourteenth and then another at the last, which was the result of his playing safe rather than taking any risks. A long drive, almost pin high left, found a barish lie and he felt it prudent to aim his putt well left of the flag for fear of rolling off into the Valley of Sin. From there he holed a putt of much the same length with which he had begun his round.

Michael Allen led the first day until taking three putts at the last hole to tie with Norman. Among eight players joint fourth with 68s were (clockwise from top right) Christy O'Connor, Jr, Ian Baker-Finch and Martin Poxon.

Nick Faldo responds to a tremendous ovation after his pitch for an eagle at the eighteenth.

Michael Allen, having won the Scottish Open a year earlier, has since qualified for the American tour, though he is still trying to find his feet. It was one of those days when everything went right for him. Even after tangling with a couple of gorse bushes in the first three holes, he still came out with par. He made another escape from a bunker at the sixth and with birdies at the seventh and ninth to add to the three he had at the first, he was out in 33.

Making the most of his luck, Allen completed the loop in level threes and then made it seven in a row at the thirteenth, where he holed from at least 100 feet, the longest putt of his life and going so fast that when it hit the back of the hole, it hopped straight up into the air before dropping back in. With yet another birdie at the fourteenth, where he was over the back in two, Allen had the chance of the lead on his own. A little sadly, he was to take three putts at the last and that brought him back alongside Norman.

Nick Faldo, after his victory in the Masters and near-miss in the American Open, when he was within an 8-foot putt of a tie, carried with him much expectation and he very much lived up to it by chasing Norman, who was only three groups ahead of him. Similarly he took his time, out in 35, but then made three birdies in the space of four holes from the tenth. This was more like it, but his high placing on the eventual leaderboard owed something to a stroke of good fortune. Driving up the eighteenth, Faldo was left with a little pitch which he played more as a chip and run with his eight iron and holed it for an eagle-two.

Ian Woosnam heightened the British interest with his 68, it soon being clear that he was in little or no discomfort with his back. He had three birdies going to the turn, interrupted only by three putts at the sixth, and two more coming home. Woosnam remarked later that if he continued to play like that, he would be there, or thereabouts, at the finish. Like Faldo had said earlier, Woosnam just wants to be in there with a shout come the last round.

With Craig Parry matching Woosnam's 68 – though it should have been better for he was undone by the closing holes – Curtis Strange had to play third fiddle with a 74. Putting is his problem these

days but if the two-time American champion was disappointed, so too was Mark Calcavecchia, even though he had managed a 71. 'A bunch of rotten golf by my book,' he said. 'The only decent iron shot I hit was at the seventeenth and that went on the road. I seemed to spend all day trying not to three-putt from 50 feet.'

When in 1984 Baker-Finch led the Open going into the final round, he began by pitching into the Swilcan Burn. That little score he promptly wiped out with a birdie en route to a 68. There were two shots dropped, one of them at the seventeenth which, as always, took its toll. Worse were the sixes taken by Peter Jacobsen and Severiano Ballesteros. Jacobsen had earlier made five birdies in a row from the third, but still did no better than a 68, largely because he could make nothing of the par fives. The Spaniard was round in 71, which he thought was about the worst he could have done.

However, Ballesteros was just one of those who thought in terms of might-have-beens. The main thing was that for once it was the top players who had formed early ranks rather than, as is often the case at this early stage, the lesser-knowns.

No one expected that these five favourites would not survive the 36-hole cut (clockwise from top left): Tom Kite, Mark Calcavecchia, Tom Watson, Severiano Ballesteros and Curtis Strange.

The first game of Jeff Woodland, Martin Poxon and David A. Russell sets off at 7.15a.m.

Some of the players' wives (above) participated in a fashion show. Daniel Sedumedi (bottom left) was making his first trip to Britain to caddie for Gary Player (right).

FIRST ROUND RESULTS

HOLE	1	2	3	4	5	6	7	8	9	10	11	12	13	14	15	16	17	18	4TOTAL
PAR	4	4	4	4	5	4	4	3	4	4	3	4	4	5	4	4	4	4	4TOTAL
Greg Norman	3	4	4	4	4	4	4	3	4	3	3	3	4	4	4	4	4	3	66
Michael Allen	3	4	4	4	5	4	3	3	3	3	3	3	3	4	4	4	4	5	66
Nick Faldo	4	4	4	4	4	4	4	3	4	3	3	3	3	5	4	4	5	2	67
Martin Poxon	3	5	4	4	5	4	3	3	4	3	3	4	4	4	4	4	3	4	68
Christy O'Connor, Jr.	3	4	3	4	4	4	4	3	4	3	3	4	5	4	4	5	4		68
Ian Baker-Finch	3	5	4	4	4	4	4	2	3	3	3	4	5	4	4	5	3		68
Craig Parry	4	3	3	3	4	4	4	3	4	3	3	3	5	3	5	6	4		68
Ian Woosnam	4	4	4	3	5	3	5	3	3	4	3	3	4	5	4	3	4	4	68
Payne Stewart	4	4	3	4	5	4	4	3	3	4	3	3	4	5	4	3	5	3	68
Peter Jacobsen	4	4	3	3	4	3	3	3	4	3	4	3	5	4	4	4	6	4	68
Sam Torrance	4	4	3	4	4	4	4	3	4	4	3	4	4	3	4	4	4		68

HOLE SUMMARY

HOLE	PAR	EAGLES	BIRDIES	PARS	BOGEYS	HIGHER	RANK	AVERAGE
1	4	1	29	102	21	3	11	3.97
2	4	0	17	99	34	6	4	4.19
3	4	1	42	104	9	0	18	3.78
4	4	0	11	92	50	3	2	4.29
5	5	2	53	86	14	1	17	4.74
6	4	0	12	119	21	4	7	4.12
7	4	0	19	112	24	1	8	4.04
8	3	0	8	124	24	0	6	3.10
9	4	0	38	106	10	2	16	3.85
OUT	36	4	229	944	207	20		36.08
10	4	0	34	109	13	0	14	3.87
11	3	0	16	98	38	4	3	3.21
12	4	0	35	97	22	2	12	3.94
13	4	0	8	119	27	2	5	4.15
14	5	1	49	79	23	4	13	4.87
15	4	0	15	124	16	1	9	4.02
16	4	0	24	111	21	0	10	3.98
17	4	0	5	65	65	21	1	4.69
18	4	1	31	112	12	0	14	3.87
IN	36	2	217	914	237	34		36.60
TOTAL	72	6	446	1858	444	54		72.68

Players Below Par	50			
Players At Par	30			
Players Above Par	76			

LOW SCORES

Low First Nine	Peter Jacobsen	31
Low Second Nine	Nick Faldo	32
	Greg Norman	32
Low Round	Michael Allen	66
	Greg Norman	66

How not to play the Road Hole and how to play it: Peter Jacobsen (above) and Nick Faldo.

THE MADDENING, FASCINATING ROAD HOLE

BY MARINO PARASCENZO

For one pithy view of the Road Hole, take Arnold Palmer. Back before the 1990 Open Championship, he spoke fondly of returning to St Andrews, where it all began for him in 1960. That was his first Open, this would be his last. A sentimental journey, he said. All the warm, wonderful memories. He and Winnie would be staying at Rusacks again, in the same room, even. He would have Tip Anderson to caddie again. There were Swilcan Burn and the town spires, Granny Clark's Wynd and the Valley of Sin, and all the other things that make St Andrews and the Old Course so special. He didn't mention the Road Hole.

Then in the Open, there was Peter Jacobsen, in the last round. He came tramping up the fairway at the Road Hole, arms overhead and pumping. This wasn't King Kong in triumph. The man was trying to surrender. A little while later came Nick Faldo, threatening to lap the field. But he tiptoed around the Road Hole. He conceded a bogey. A kind of sacrificial offering. Don't wake up the beast.

Funny thing about this Open, though. The Road Hole – the seventeenth – took a real beating. It gave up *fifteen* birdies. Time was you could count the birdies there on your index finger. (In the third round of the 1978 Open, for example.) And it played to an average of only 4.65 this time. The fourteenth hole played to a 4.97 average.

Maybe that's unfair to the fourteenth. After all the fourteenth is a par five. The seventeenth is a par four.

'It's a par four and a half,' says Jack Nicklaus.

'I play it for a five,' says Christy O'Connor, Jr.

'I can't play that hole, I really can't,' says Greg Norman.

Believers rejoice. Nothing has really changed. In the 1990 Open, there were four days of absolutely benign weather – warm and sunny and barely enough breeze to stir a flag. The Road Hole remained the toughest hole on the Old Course, to say nothing of Scotland, the British Isles, and the world.

Consider: Faldo won by five strokes, at eighteen under par. But he didn't birdie the seventeenth. He didn't even really try. Even with a hot hand, he wasn't about to challenge it. A tightrope is no place to start tap-dancing. Faldo said he more or less played the seventeenth as a par five. That being the case, he stole a stroke: five-four-five-five.

What is it that makes actuaries cringe?

Well, as golf holes go, it doesn't look like much. Certainly nothing like its reputation. A scary golf hole ought to look scary. Take the twelfth at Augusta National, sitting behind that placid pool, with the breezes sighing high in the trees overhead. It's a beauty, if you like scorpions. Then there's the famed sixteenth at Cypress Point, the hole with the built-in solution. A couple hundred yards across a chasm with the Pacific Ocean frothing at its feet below. You can always jump. 'When I step on that tee,' American golfer, Bob Gilder said, 'the blood drains out of my legs.' Now, there's a compliment.

Now look at the Road Hole. At 461 yards, it's a bit hefty for a par four, and that seems to be it. No raging ocean, no beckoning trees, no hills to climb, no hairpin-turn doglegs. It's like a lovable old sheepdog stretched out for a snooze.

Actually, it's maddening, is what it is. Delicious, refined psychological terror. This is the Bermuda Triangle of golf. For a start, it's disorienting. You can't get your bearings. It looks like a dogleg, but it's actually straight, until you get to your second shot, which you think is straight, but it's a dogleg, the way the green cants to the left. Of course, you can play it as a dogleg off the tee if you like. The option is there, but the odds aren't. You would think this hole was designed by a committee. But the hole wasn't designed by anyone. It just happened.

'If an architect had designed it,' Henry Cotton once said, 'they would have asked for their money back.'

Peter Thomson, five-times Open champion, wasn't so kind. Whoever would design such a hole today, he said, would be sued for incompetence.

There is an old joke that must have been about the Road Hole. A travelling salesman asks the village idiot for directions. 'Well, you go five blocks that way, then turn left. . . No, you go three blocks this way and turn right. . . No, you. . . Well,' the idiot says, 'the thing is, you can't get there from here.' You can't get to the Road Hole either.

There are two ways to try. First, straightaway. The drive must carry the edge of the Old Course Hotel grounds directly ahead. That's out of bounds, over the wall. So don't bite off too much wall, don't slice, and do pray the wind doesn't blow. Some aim over the reproductions of the original railroad sheds on the hotel grounds. Some, like Jack Nicklaus, aim at a spire in town. Some aim at a cloud the caddie has pointed out. Maybe some just close their eyes and swing.

Then there is the dogleg route. The tee shot goes well to the left, safely away from the hotel grounds. Now for the approach. This brings the bunker right into the line of fire.

Did anybody mention the bunker? You can say it's the only hazard on the Road Hole, because it is. But that's like saying the Grand Canyon is a gulley in Arizona. This is the Road Bunker. It's where Dante went down to do research for the Inferno.

The Road Bunker is the true source of the Road Hole's power, the nerve centre, the generator. The bunker shoves its way into the left midsection of the green. The floor is an oval, about 14 feet wide, 11 feet front to back. On the fairway side to the left, it's at ground level. The ball can roll right in. To the right, where it rises up to the green, it's about 5 feet deep and straight-faced. The average man has the top of the bunker at shoulder height, and he's trying to splash the ball out to a flag he can almost touch. There are any number of ways to get into the bunker.

You can roll it in, fly it in, putt in from the front, chip in from any side. That's why you're either playing the Road Hole or thinking about it. You're not safe from the bunker until the ball is in the hole.

The green, on a plateau about 3 feet high, is something like an aircraft carrier coming about to port. It's immense, some 60 yards long, but if you're trying to get where the flagstick is (and the bunker), you're hitting at a space only 43 feet wide. You are trying to thread a needle from 200 yards.

Miss to the left, and you are either in the bunker or you have to play around it or over it. Miss to the right by about 10 feet, and you are on the road that gives the hole its name. And the road is in play. Miss farther to the right, and you are up against a stone wall 5 feet high. Some think they have the secret. These are the same people who found Atlantis.

'What you need there,' said 1989 Open champion, Mark Calcavecchia, who plays a fade, 'is a big, sweeping hook to get at the pin.'

'You have that shot, don't you?' Tom Kite said, feeding him the straight line.

'Sure,' Calcavecchia said. 'But I just don't know when.'

In practice for the 1990 Open, Calcavecchia went after the hole with his big, sweeping fade. He birdied it. Then he bogeyed it in the first round, parred it in the second, and missed the thirty-six hole cut.

There is a right way to play the Road Hole, and a wrong way. The 1984 Open gave us dramatic textbook cases, within moments of each other.

Severiano Ballesteros, in the next-to-last pairing, played it the wrong way. He drove far to the left, into the rough. Then he hit a six iron 203 yards to the front of the green, and two-putted from transcontinental distance for his par. At least it saved him a return visit. He had bogeyed the hole three days running, and he vowed that if he didn't par it in the final round, he would come back on Monday.

Tom Watson, the leader, was in the last pairing, and he played it the right way. He hit a drawing board tee shot over the hotel grounds. But then his two iron bounced across the road and ended up almost against the wall. He made a brilliant bogey from there, and lost. Ballesteros made a brilliant par, and won the

Open. Watson played the Road Hole the wrong way. Ballesteros played it the right way. See?

But not in the first round of the 1990 Open. Ballesteros drove into the same left rough again. His seven iron twisted on a clump of grass, his wedge hit near the pin and rolled away, and he three-putted for a six.

'Do I like seventeen?' he said. 'Do you want me to say it is a bad hole, after what happened in 1984? It is a *great* hole, something you always remember when you play. It is the toughest par four in the world.'

('It's the toughest par four in the world,' Ben Crenshaw has said, 'because it's a par five.')

Peter Jacobsen must hold some kind of distinction for double bogeys farthest apart. He double-bogeyed the Road Hole in the final round of the 1984 Open, then double-bogeyed it again in the first round of the 1990 Open. He broke the monotony in the second round. He got one of those fifteen birdies. And he *knew* it was coming, if that tells you anything about the hole.

First, he slipped past the guards with his drive. 'You can go much farther to the right than you think,' he said. Then he hit a bump-and-run four iron that bumped but wouldn't run. It stopped on the low front shelf of the green. He was facing a putt of about 75 feet.

'I hardly looked at the line,' Jacobsen said. 'I knew it was going in. My caddie is thinking, "I hope he keeps it on the green," and I told him to go up to the pin and get the ball out of the hole.'

Jacobsen is no mind reader. Everybody thinks the same when the ball is on the front. Probably the most fun for the thousands of spectators, in the stands beyond the wall to the right, is the putt from the front, past the bunker. That putt must follow the precise line and have the precise speed in order to defy gravity. The bunker, shoved into the side of the green from the left, heaves up a big shoulder that the ball has to ride. A little too far left or a little too slow, and the bunker sucks it down. That's what happened to Tommy Nakajima in the 1978 Open, in the third round, when he was just a few strokes off the lead. It took him four to get out of the bunker, three putts to get down, and he had a nine. The bunker is also known as 'The Sands of Nakajima'.

None of that for Jacobsen. His putt broke about 12 feet to the right, 8 feet to the left. The caddie looked at him. Then took the ball out of the cup.

And in the last round, we found Jacobsen coming up the fairway, arms lifted. This time he had driven too far left, and he was trying to hack his way out of the rough. He had come to the Road Hole three under par for the day. A par would have put him in seventh place, a bogey maybe in eighth place. But he made an eight, for a 73, and finished joint sixteenth.

James Spence, a young British golfer, got into the Open through the qualifying rounds. This was his first Open, and his first visit to St Andrews. Why the fuss over the Road Hole? He hit the green the first day and two-putted for a par. The second day, he hit a five iron 188 yards, to 8 feet, and holed the putt for one of the fifteen birdies – in a round of 65. 'I like that hole at the moment,' Spence said. The moment ended when he bogeyed it the next two rounds.

American Jodie Mudd, also making his first visit to St Andrews, will have something to tell his grandchildren. On his way to a 66 in the second round, he drove into the left rough, and couldn't move his six-iron second shot more than 10 yards. Then he hit an eight iron that ended up on the road, about 70 feet from the flag. He pitched to 6 feet and holed the putt for a terrific five. Then Mudd was on a tear in the last round. He was seven under par, with eight birdies and one bogey. Then he double-bogeyed the seventeenth. A birdie at the eighteenth gave him another 66 and a tie for fourth.

Mark McNulty logged a great par in the final round. It was the Road Hole personified. And he never even saw it.

He was confused. He couldn't decide whether to hit his approach to the left or to the right. He ended up on the road. 'It was teed up on a couple of stones, though,' he said. He pitched on with his wedge, only to become confused again. The putt would break left-to-right, or was it right-to-left? 'So I hit it straight,' he said. But he couldn't bear to look. He turned away. 'I heard it drop,' he said.

Wires cross, fuses blow. The Road Hole exerts that kind of force.

Nick Faldo matched Sir Henry Cotton's 1934 record and his scores.

2

NORMAN, FALDO SET A MEMORABLE PACE

BY MICHAEL WILLIAMS

In my twenty years of covering the Open Championship for the *Daily Telegraph*, two days remain indelibly etched in my memory. They were at Turnberry in 1977 when, over the final two rounds, Tom Watson and Jack Nicklaus, the two finest golfers of their time, fought it out toe-to-toe to the exclusion of everyone else, so much so that when Hubert Green came third, ten strokes behind, he described himself as 'the winner of the other tournament.' The main bout of the true heavyweights went to Watson, who already that year had beaten Nicklaus in a tight finish for the Masters, and now did so again after some golf that it was hard to see ever being eclipsed.

Tied at the halfway stage, each with rounds of 68 and 70, they were still tied after the third as each scored 65 before Watson won with another 65 to a 66 by Nicklaus. It set a championship record of 268 which stands to this day.

But, here at St Andrews, the game's ultimate stage, there came something to stand alongside those two epic days. Greg Norman and Nick Faldo, whose standing in the game is almost exactly parallel to that of Watson and Nicklaus thirteen years ago, fought a mirror image of that classic duel at Turnberry. Norman, who has always promised so much more than he has achieved, repeated his first round of 66 and yet it failed to break Faldo, who now followed his 67 with a 65 so that at the halfway point they were tied on 132, twelve under par, and four strokes clear of the field. Of course, it had to be taken in the context that this was only the second round and there were still thirty-six holes to play but, by heavens, it was something to be savoured.

Here were two supreme golfers, every nerve and sinew at stretching point, summoning the very best they could produce. And all this on the very shores of St Andrews Bay, where the first shots to the opening sequence of that classic film, *Chariots of Fire*, were made. Somehow one could see something of Harold Abrahams in Faldo, just as one could also see something of Eric Liddell in Norman. All one needed was the orchestra to strike up.

By setting a pace of 132 for the thirty-six holes, Norman and Faldo equalled the record of Henry Cotton at Royal St George's in 1934. Faldo indeed repeated Cotton's 67, 65. One record, however, was smashed altogether. On another day of almost cruelly low scoring, the guillotine that is the halfway cut fell at 143, one under par, and three strokes lower than it had ever been before. It was cruel because of the casualties it caused and to one in particular, Arnold Palmer.

At the age of sixty, Palmer had come for one last Open at the very place where, thirty years ago, he had arrived for the Centenary Championship. Palmer was then the King, winner that year of both the Masters, for a second time, and the US Open for a first, but the treble eluded him as Kel Nagle, of Australia, beat him by a shot. Palmer was, nevertheless, hooked and came back to win the next year at Royal Birkdale and the next at Troon. As a result an Open Championship that had at the time lost its place in the game was back where it belonged.

If there were those who suspected that Palmer's last bow would be a token one, they could not have been more wrong. He was still smarting from the two 82s he had at Royal Troon a year ago and now, summoning something of his past genius, he had scores of 73 and 71. In all the previous years of the Open, that would have easily been good enough. Now it was not. He was level par, but out of the championship.

Yet at the time Palmer came off the eighteenth green he believed he was safe. Striding from the thirteenth green he calculated that he needed one more birdie and he got it at the fifteenth, a six iron to 10 feet. 'The galleries were fantastic,' he said afterwards. 'They sensed the same thing I was feeling and that was really to push myself and I think they felt the same relief when I finished with two fours for 71. I could almost feel the vibrations from the crowd as I was walking up the last hole.'

Regrettably, it was not to be, but Palmer was not alone as a former champion to take an early exit. So did Mark Calcavecchia, the holder, who followed his 71 with a 75, and Severiano Ballesteros, who had won here in 1984, but now took 71 and 74. Tom Watson (72, 73) was out, so was Gary Player (72, 73), Tom Weiskopf (73, 74) and Bob Charles (76, 75) – seven former champions in all. In addition to them, Curtis Strange's 74 and 71 was another example of his inability to include his American game amongst his luggage.

Faldo made a good point that he and Norman had opened up such a large lead that the pressure was now off those immediately behind them, leaving them free to make an assault without the pressure he and Norman were under. 'A long way to go,' he said. With Payne Stewart and Craig Parry, both with two rounds of 68 behind them, the closest in touch, anything could yet happen.

Lined up behind them were Nick Price, who has twice come close to winning this championship. He had only recently recovered from a broken finger which forced him to miss the US Open a month earlier. Also, there were Ian Woosnam, Mike Reid, who had nearly won the American PGA Championship the previous year, and James Spence. By no means out of it either were Jose-Maria Olazabal, who had a highly impressive second round of 67, Jodie Mudd, even more impressive with a 66, Peter Jacobsen, Sam Torrance, Steve Pate and a Dane – Anders Sorensen. These last six were all on 138, six strokes behind.

Spence created the spark to this unforgettable day. He was the first man out at 7.15 a.m., the flags again limp at the mastheads, and no one paid too much attention since his first round had been a 72. But they soon did as he went to the turn in 33 despite a six at the fifth, where most were looking for birdies.

Four threes in a row from the sixth got him going. Then there was a lull before he finished with four more birdies in this last six holes, the best of them at the treacherous seventeenth. There he hit a five iron second shot 188 yards to 8 feet, holing indeed a longer putt than the one he missed for what would have been a 64 at the last. Even so, a 65 left him, for a time, on top of the leaderboards.

Having come through both the regional qualifying at Hankley Common and the final qualifying at Panmure, these were dizzy heights for Spence, who had never played in the Open before. Almost his first thought was that when his father, who had suffered a heart attack last Christmas, saw his son's name leading the way, he hopefully would not suffer another one! At age twenty-seven, Spence is still struggling to make his mark on the European tour but he has always had faith in himself and there is no better place to justify that than in the Open at St Andrews.

Spence had completed his round, gone through his press interview and had his lunch before Norman and Faldo had even begun their second rounds. It was not long before they were in full cry, though there was an early slip by Norman when he took three putts at the second, admittedly from 40 feet. However, he got it back at the fourth, quite a long par four but downwind and now needing only an eight-iron second. With a run of three, two, three, three from the seventh he was pressurizing Faldo who, thirty minutes behind him, was nevertheless keeping pace with four birdies in his first seven holes, three of them in a row from the fifth.

While Norman claims not to pay particular attention to the leaderboards, he must have been aware of what was going on behind him. When he missed the thirteenth green, not seriously for he was still able to putt but took five, one wondered whether his head might go down. It did not because he immediately had a stroke of extreme good fortune, of the sort that Faldo had at the eighteenth in the first round when he holed his second shot for a two.

A drive and three wood down the fourteenth was not sufficient, into the wind, to get Norman home in two and he was left with a pitch of 75 yards over the hump that climbs steeply at the mouth of the green.

He then played the most lovely high pitch, his ball dropping a yard behind the flag and spinning back into the hole for an eagle-three. What a moment it was, and no one could have been anything but pleased for Norman, who has seen this sort of thing done to him more often than he has done it to others. The strain seemed to ebb away and with a birdie at the sixteenth, the Australian was home in 33 for a 66.

Meanwhile, Faldo, out in 32, had made a fifth birdie at the tenth with his third long putt of the round, this time 18 feet, but he was two behind after Norman's three at the sixteenth. However, no golfer in the world today has more resolve and Faldo simply refused to be shaken. Orthodox par followed orthodox par, with the exception of the thirteenth, where from much the same place that Norman had putted, he chipped to keep his head above water. The reward came at the fifteenth and sixteenth. There

Faldo played two glorious second shots, a six iron through a cross wind to 2 feet and then a seven iron to 4 feet. Each time he sank the putts for birdies. Though he had to work for his four at the seventeenth, he was back in 33 for a 65 to tie the lead.

Norman said he was disappointed with his five at the thirteenth, 'because I did not hit a poor shot'. But he was enthusiastic about his golf and particularly about his putting, having the feeling that he could hole anything. For all that, he claimed not to be at all excited, 'just happy, comfortable and relaxed.' He would continue to play, he said, his normal game. Faldo thought the key had been in going the turn in 32 because everyone was making progress and he knew he could not afford to lose ground.

Payne Stewart, in the colours of the Green Bay Packers, one of the twenty-eight teams he represents from the National Football League of America, kept

Caddie Fanny Sunneson and Faldo scan the flight of one of his shots in the second round.

his end up with a second 68. His only slip was a five at the twelfth, where he drove into one of the many bunkers that litter the fairway like a minefield. Otherwise, it was another impeccable performance with the bonus of retrieving a four at the seventeenth, where he managed to get down in two despite having to negotiate the 'wall of death' that can lead to the Road Bunker. Parry matched him step for step, making up the most ground in an outward half of 32. A sound putting stroke had, he felt, put less pressure on the rest of his game.

Ian Woosnam was going very well with an outward half of 32 and then two more birdies at the tenth and eleventh, where he holed from only 2 feet. He was then ten under par for the championship and right in the thick of the fight. However, he drove into the rough right of the fifteenth fairway to drop a stroke and then fell foul of the seventeenth, finding the Road Bunker with his second shot. So much depends on where you are in that bunker and Woosnam, not well placed, had to play out well wide of the flag and then three-putted, missing something of a tiddler. He was not a happy man, dropping back from a potential third place to a share of fifth with Spence, Nick Price and Mike Reid, the last two both round in 67.

Price was particularly pleased because he had been suffering some loss of form after breaking his finger on an outboard motor. It was mostly his putting which suffered, but he had since straightened it out and though there was still some room for improvement in his iron play, at least his driving was leaving him in the right position from which he could attack the flags. Reid, thrilled to be playing at St Andrews for the first time, was delighted to be so well up after taking a six at the seventeenth in the first round. He realized the importance here of being patient. Mudd's 66 could easily have been better than that, for he was seven under par after fourteen holes, but dropped shots at both the sixteenth and seventeenth, where he was in all manner of trouble and could easily, he said, have had an eight. He got down in two from off the road.

There was a strong move as well from Jose-Maria Olazabal, now with a 67 that drew some very favourable comments from Jack Nicklaus, his part-ner through the first two rounds. 'For two days he knocked the flagsticks out of the hole,' said Nicklaus. But the difference in this second round was the putting, a very variable department of the game so far as the young Spaniard is concerned these days. What he had managed to do, nevertheless, was rescue a game that had deserted him the previous week when he surprisingly missed the cut in the Scottish Open. To find it again he had spent the whole of Wednesday on the practice ground and sacrificing, therefore, a final practice round.

Faldo and Norman had got their timing right too and the golfing world sat back to await their confrontation with baited breath. Two momentous days lay ahead to decide who really was the world's best golfer.

Payne Stewart's putting kept him in touch with the leaders on 136 after two rounds.

James Spence (below) was first out in the second round and set the spark for the day with a 65. Ronan Rafferty (bottom right) was safely under par on 141, while Ian Woosnam (bottom left) was on 137 and Craig Parry (top left) was joint third on 136.

Next page, Anders Sorensen (top left) and Peter Jacobsen (top right) were among those on 138, while Amateur champions Rolf Muntz (bottom left) and Chris Patton (bottom right) missed the 36-hole cut.

SECOND ROUND RESULTS

HOLE	1	2	3	4	5	6	7	8	9	10	11	12	13	14	15	16	17	18	
PAR	4	4	4	4	5	4	4	3	4	4	3	4	4	5	4	4	4	4	4 TOTAL
Greg Norman	4	5	4	3	5	4	3	2	3	3	3	4	5	3	4	3	4	4	66-132
Nick Faldo	4	3	4	4	4	3	3	3	4	3	3	4	4	5	3	3	4	4	65-132
Payne Stewart	3	4	4	4	4	3	4	3	4	4	2	5	4	4	4	4	4	4	68-136
Craig Parry	4	4	3	4	4	3	3	3	4	4	2	4	5	4	4	4	5	4	68-136
James Spence	3	4	4	4	6	3	3	3	3	4	3	4	3	4	4	3	3	4	65-137
Nick Price	3	4	4	4	4	4	4	3	4	3	2	4	4	5	3	4	4	4	67-137
Mike Reid	4	4	4	4	3	3	4	3	4	4	3	4	3	4	3	5	4	4	67-137
Ian Woosnam	4	3	3	4	5	3	3	3	4	3	2	4	4	5	5	4	6	4	69-137
J-M Olazabal	4	4	3	4	5	3	4	3	4	3	3	4	4	5	4	3	4	3	67-138
Jodie Mudd	3	3	4	4	4	4	4	2	3	4	3	3	4	4	4	5	5	3	66-138
Peter Jacobsen	5	3	3	4	4	4	4	3	4	4	3	4	4	5	4	5	3	4	70-138
Sam Torrance	4	5	3	3	4	3	5	3	4	4	3	4	5	5	4	4	4	3	70-138
Steve Pate	4	4	5	3	5	4	3	3	3	3	3	3	4	5	4	5	3	4	68-138
Anders Sorensen	4	3	4	4	3	5	3	3	3	3	3	4	4	5	4	4	5	4	68-138

HOLE SUMMARY

HOLE	PAR	EAGLES	BIRDIES	PARS	BOGEYS	HIGHER	RANK	AVERAGE
1	4	0	52	95	7	2	16	3.74
2	4	0	25	97	30	4	5	4.08
3	4	0	41	105	9	1	14	3.81
4	4	0	11	115	29	1	3	4.13
5	5	5	67	73	11	0	17	4.58
6	4	0	33	103	19	1	10	3.92
7	4	0	31	95	28	2	6	4.01
8	3	0	19	127	9	1	9	2.95
9	4	1	34	111	10	0	13	3.83
OUT	36	6	313	921	152	12		35.05
10	4	1	59	88	8	0	18	3.66
11	3	0	19	128	9	0	10	2.94
12	4	1	24	119	12	0	12	3.91
13	4	0	6	83	57	10	2	4.46
14	5	1	36	92	21	6	7	4.97
15	4	0	22	118	15	1	8	3.97
16	4	0	22	101	30	3	4	4.09
17	4	0	8	73	63	12	1	4.55
18	4	0	36	114	6	0	14	3.81
IN	36	3	232	916	221	32		36.36
TOTAL	72	9	545	1837	373	44		71.41

Surprisingly, Rodger Davis (left) and Craig Stadler (right) were at the bottom of the field.

Players Below Par	86
Players At Par	17
Players Above Par	53

LOW SCORES		
Low First Nine	Jorge Berendt	31
	Jodie Mudd	31
Low Second Nine	James Spence	32
Low Round	Nick Faldo	65
	James Spence	65

Arnold Palmer was returning to St Andrews thirty years after his first Open Championship.

ARNIE, WILL YE NO' COME BACK AGAIN?

BY ALISTER NICOL

As a child growing up in the town of Latrobe, Pennsylvania, Arnold Palmer's first real interest was aircraft. The son of the golf professional and greenkeeper at the local golf club, Palmer spent hour after hour messing around with glue, bits of wire and pieces of wood. Aircraft absolutely fascinated him. Yet he was, in his own words, frightened nearly to death by his maiden flight. His subsequent reaction, however, was an early indication of the drive and resolve which were to carry him to the pinnacle of success.

The terror induced by wheeling in the skies in a small bi-plane merely inspired him to become even more interested in what made a man-made machine defy gravity and soar free above the earth. Palmer conquered that early fear to such an extent that some years ago he set a world record in a business jet. By then, he had also conquered the world of golf and the hearts of millions of golf watchers worldwide to whom the words 'Arnie' and 'golf' were synonymous.

British golf fans knew little in 1960 of Arnold Daniel Palmer, other than when he arrived at St Andrews for the Centenary Open he did so as winner of the Masters in Augusta, Georgia, and the US Open at Cherry Hills in Denver, Colorado, that same year. He had also partnered Sam Snead to win the World Cup for the United States at Portmarnock.

Indeed, up to the point he and wife, Winnie, arrived at St Andrews by overnight sleeper from London, 1960 had been a great year for Palmer, hero of American golf galleries with his all-out attacking style from tee to green allied to a putting touch as deft and sure as a neuro-surgeon with a scalpel.

The thirty-year-old Palmer had the common touch as he hitched his trousers in a fashion which was to become as much his on-course trade mark as John Wayne's walk was to Western movies. As befits someone at the very peak of his career, Palmer went into the Centenary Open almost counting it as his own even before the first ball was struck.

It was his first foray overseas, and his arrival in 1960 was overdue as far as Palmer was concerned. Golf had gradually superseded model plane-making and as a teenager Palmer's golfing talent rapidly grew and matured. Part of the growing up and learning process was to devour every book upon which he could lay his hands and he was soon aware of the rich history of the game that Scottish emigrants had taken with them across the Atlantic as they fled the economic hardships of the early 1900s for America.

Before he turned professional at the age of twenty-five, it had been Palmer's dream to cross the Atlantic the other way to compete in the Amateur Championship. However, he also encountered economic strictures and had to wait until he was Masters and US Open champion before making his first British Isles landfall. The last player to have won those two titles before going to Scotland to win the Open, golf's oldest championship, had been Ben Hogan in 1953. He won at Carnoustie, a few miles across the Firth of Tay from St Andrews.

For one reason or another, few top-flight Americans returned after Hogan's win and the Open suffered something of a decline. A concerned Palmer spotted what was going on. 'I had watched what had happened to the Open and felt that it really was one of golf's truly major championships and ought to be recognized as such. That's why I decided to go for the Centenary Open,' he recalled at St Andrews in 1990. 'And one of the greatest disappointments of my entire career is that I did not win that year.'

He felt he could have and should have won, and will always insist that only the elements robbed him of the Open title at his first attempt thirty years ago.

'I really did think I was going to win,' Palmer said. 'Without taking anything at all from Kel Nagle, who beat me by one shot, I felt — and still feel — I should have won but I didn't, and I guess that's the name of the game. I played well, my putting was not good and that was part of the story. But I have always blamed the rain interruption for my not winning.

'I felt if we had completed the thirty-six holes that afternoon, as was the case in those days, I would have won. I was ready. I was fired up and felt I would play well. I did play well the next day to shoot 68, but not as well as I would have done had we played on through the Friday afternoon.'

A memory as vivid as his disappointment was the sight from his room in Rusacks Hotel of rainwater cascading down the steps of the R&A Clubhouse and flooding the Valley of Sin, the depression in front of the eighteenth green, to a depth of three feet. Never for a moment did he think play in the Open would be called off for rain. But it was, and that cloudburst swept away his dreams of success.

That only heightened his resolve to team up again with the caddie he met for the first time that year – Tip Anderson, a St Andrean born and bred, a single-figure player and one who knew the Old Course and her capricious moods well. Palmer had asked the R&A to find him just such a man, and the partnership grew into a firm friendship.

Palmer had such respect for Anderson that when hip problems precluded him from returning for the 1964 Open Championship, he not only gave winner Tony Lema his putter, he gave him Tip as well.

Lema was one of the many fellow Americans whom Palmer, in his role as recruiting sergeant as well as supreme commander of Arnie's Army, talked into resuscitating the Open. 'I told Lema and all the others that if they wanted to take their place among the greats in golf and keep it, they had to come to Britain and win at least one Open,' Palmer said.

The fact that Arnold won at Royal Birkdale in 1961 and successfully defended the following year at Troon encouraged his recruiting drive. By then, of course, golf had attracted a vast following through television, and nobody was better equipped than Arnold for a starring role.

His impact on the course was more than matched by his appeal off it and his patent honesty, his natural charm, his all-American image drew advertising men like pins to a magnet. The kid who used to make model planes could now afford his own. The kid who was not allowed to swim in the pool at Latrobe Country Club where his father was professional, bought the whole place, and still didn't swim in the pool.

He kept coming to the Open and was such an attraction that the R&A, grateful, yet fearful that one day he would stop making the pilgrimage, kept finding ways to ensure his exemption from having to pre-qualify.

As long ago as 1984, Arnold told me in his office at his Bay Hill Club and Lodge in Orlando, Florida – an office festooned by model airplanes – that his trip for that year's Open would probably be his last. But he played at Muirfield two years later, and again at Royal Troon last year when he shot 82, 82 to finish last. And therein lies the tale of why he chose St Andrews 1990 to make his swan-song.

While failure to win over the Old Course in 1960 will always be his biggest disappointment, his Troon efforts come a close second. Over a course where he had won an Open in similar conditions in 1962, his golf in 1989 fell far below the standards he set himself, even with his sixtieth birthday on the horizon.

When he left St Andrews in 1960 he promised himself he would return to Britain to win an Open. When he left Troon twenty-nine years later he said he would probably not return to the Open. Then his pride began to nag at him. He changed his mind and worked to tune his game to just about the finest pitch he could achieve, and decided to have one more crack.

'I wanted to redeem myself with at least two good rounds,' he said after shooting 73, 71 which, early on the Friday of the Open, looked good to make the cut. In the end that effort, in which he covered his last six holes in level fours, failed by one stroke.

He hid that hurt well from all but a few friends, and slipped quietly away to Turnberry to prepare for the seniors tournament there. His disappointment at missing the last two days of the 1990 Open was more than matched by that of the record-breaking galleries

who had cheered every shot of his first two rounds.

Like Arnold, they had expected his level-par total of 144 to qualify, and they went home on Friday content that come the Sunday they would give their hero a send-off he would never forget.

Thousands were all set to sing *Will Ye No' Come Back Again* as he marched up the eighteenth fairway with Anderson at his shoulder. He confessed to a few lumps in his throat as a result of his reception on Thursday and Friday. And, the great traditionalist may have proved himself a sentimentalist and shed a few tears had the chorus had their chance on Sunday. Friends and fans were cheated by the lowest-ever cut-off point in Open history, a history which Arnold Palmer enriched in an unrivalled sporting manner over three decades.

Now, however, at the age of sixty, Palmer feels there is little more he can do for the championship he revived virtually single-handed.

'Of course I have regrets about not coming back, sure I have,' he said. 'But I have to be realistic and accept the situation that I will be sixty-one years old next year and I feel like it is time to not play in the Open any more.

'I have had thirty good years of the Open and I have enjoyed it. I have enjoyed the courses, enjoyed the people and made a lot of friends. I have won it a couple of times and come close a few more times and done all the things I set out to do all those years ago. I have seen it grow from the St Andrews of thirty years ago to the St Andrews of 1990. There is not much more I can do to help the Open. It is off and running now and this is a nice time to say goodbye.'

When Arnold and Winnie Palmer arrived at St Andrews in 1960, it was by public transport. When they left in 1990, it was by private jet. The modes of transport were as far apart as Antarctica and Alaska but the passengers were still the same good, honest, decent people who will be sorely missed by every spectator and television viewer who has watched an Open these last thirty years.

Arnie and Winnie, will ye no' come back again?

The anticipated duel between Nick Faldo and Greg Norman became a one-man show.

DAY

3

NICK GOES FIVE STROKES CLEAR

BY MICHAEL WILLIAMS

In boxing terms it was no contest. Ever since Friday evening the golfing world had waited for the two best players in the game, Greg Norman and Nick Faldo, in that order according to the Sony world rankings, to climb into the ring that was the first tee at St Andrews for their classic confrontation that, still in the terms of the pugilists, was scheduled to go another two rounds. It was all over in one, however, for while Faldo ascended further heights, adding a 67 to the 67 and 65 he had on the previous two days, Norman, with whom he had been tied after thirty-six holes, went out for the count with a 76.

It was not so much a case of how well Faldo had played, the first man in the history of the Open to break, with 199, the 200 barrier for the fifty-four holes, but how badly Norman had performed just when he had the chance to prove that beneath those handsome looks, flaxen hair and a dashing swing there really was a man of steel.

Norman had carried the image of someone who had never quite gotten the rewards his marvellous striking of the golf ball deserved, almost of someone who was indeed born under an unlucky star. Only twelve months earlier at Royal Troon there had been a brilliant last round of 64 which got him into a play-off. Then he hit such a monumental drive at the fourth extra hole that he reached a bunker even he thought was out of reach so that he handed the title, which everyone thought was his, to Mark Calcavecchia.

There was also the 1986 American PGA Championship he lost when Bob Tway holed a bunker shot at the last; the chip Larry Mize sank to beat him at the second extra hole in the 1987 Masters; two other Masters when he faltered only with his second shots to the last; the 1984 American Open he lost in a play-off to Fuzzy Zoeller; and the seven iron earlier

in the year which Robert Gamez holed to beat him at the slightly lesser level of the Bay Hill tournament. No one can get much more unfortunate than that.

Even so, there must have been shots on all these occasions which Norman could have replayed with much more success and never let himself into the situation from which ultimately he lost. Somewhere, it seemed, there might after all have been a flaw. Now that seemed abundantly evident with the weakness of his resistance to Faldo, just as he needed to be at his strongest. One wonders how long those wounds will take to heal or whether, indeed, they will heal at all. Careers do have their turning points.

Faldo graciously said that for Norman it was one of those days when nothing went right – apparently good shots getting some unkind kick, putts which had previously gone in now missing. But the fact remains that the Australian Adonis failed almost lamentably to live up to his reputation. An always gracious loser and the most considerate of players when it comes to the eternal Press grillings that follow disaster as well as triumph, Norman for once refused to be interviewed. And who could really blame him?

So, the Open had taken an unexpected turn. No longer were Faldo and Norman slugging it out in the manner of Tom Watson and Jack Nicklaus at Turnberry in 1977. Instead Faldo, so intent on revenge for the 8-foot putt he had missed to tie the US Open (which I think he would almost certainly have won to put him on line for the Grand Slam), was five strokes clear and in, for him, a position from which it was almost impossible to see him losing.

The man Faldo had perhaps most to worry about now was Payne Stewart, the reigning American PGA champion with a good record in the Open with one second place and one third, as he completed his third successive round of 68 for a total of 204. It put him alongside Ian Baker-Finch, who had played one of the two outstanding rounds of the day, a 64 to give himself a chance of making up for the other one he had missed here at St Andrews in 1984.

Another Australian, Craig Parry, who is as short and squat as Norman and Baker-Finch are tall and lean, held his head high with his third round under 70, now a 69 for 205. He was one behind Stewart and Baker-Finch but one in front of Paul Broadhurst, who played the day's other outstanding round, a 63, which equalled the Open Championship record and was only one outside the course record.

Ian Woosnam was under par again with a 70, but that lost ground rather than gained it as he was caught for a share of sixth place by Frank Nobilo, of New Zealand, who had a 68. Next came a cluster of six, Norman among them; the others were Tim Simpson (69), Vicente Fernandez (69), Nick Price (71), Peter Jacobsen (70) and Corey Pavin (68).

There were big Scottish cheers, too, for Sandy Lyle, who had had such a miserable eighteen months but was now finding again something of his old touch with a 67, as he slowly found familiarity with some swing changes which are easier to produce on the practice ground than they are on the golf course. He had found the course playing pretty easily to the turn and predicted scores in the region of 33 or 34 for Faldo and Norman with the seventeenth, particularly if the wind stayed in the east, likely to be the key hole. 'Norman, if he gets a good start, will be hard to beat,' said Lyle, 'but I give Faldo the edge on putting.' How true the latter part of that prediction was to become!

Just as there had been sadness the day before when Arnold Palmer missed the cut, now there was more as Jack Nicklaus, twice a winner here, took 77, which was the worst round he had ever had over the Old Course. It did not leave him quite last of the seventy-two players who made the cut, but only Jose-Maria Canizares, of Spain, was below him.

Certainly the course was still vulnerable and no one proved that better than Paul Broadhurst, who not only had that 63 but went out in 29, which brought back the memories of Tony Jacklin's 29 in 1970 as he began his defence of the title he had won the previous year at Royal Lytham. Jacklin, from a

television commentary box, was there to see it, on the screen anyway. Present, too, was Doug Sanders, the man who got so much nearer to winning, missing indeed a 3-foot putt on the last green before going down to Nicklaus in the play-off. It was a visit he made for sentimental reasons, but only at the last minute.

Broadhurst was not even sure he would be playing in the third round, being on the borderline of 143 for the thirty-six holes. He had left the course some time before the cut was known on the Friday and was in the middle of dinner when he telephoned the R&A. Stepping into the old style telephone box, with its hinged door, he was caught unawares as it swung back on him and caught him on the forehead, opening a nasty little cut over his right eye. In no way could it be said to have affected his golf.

Always something of a 'streak' player, Broadhurst who had finished low amateur in the 1988 Open at Royal Lytham – where earlier that year he had won the Lytham Trophy – played some astonishing golf, out not only in 29 but then going eight under par for the first ten holes. Other than the fifth, which he two-putted for his birdie-four and a putt of 1 foot for a three at the seventh, Broadhurst sank five putts of 10 feet or more. His hottest streak was, after birdies at the first and third, coming from the fifth as he reeled off six consecutive birdies. He could remember doing that only once before.

At such point there were visions even of a 59, but with the breeze against him coming home, the going was harder for Broadhurst, and his visions of a course record began to fade. Still there was always the goal of equalling the championship record and it came at the last, a stunning nine iron to a foot. He was lucky only once, getting away with a four at the seventeenth, but otherwise it was one of those days when he simply could not see himself hitting a bad shot.

Just as Broadhurst was completing his remarkable round, so another was beginning. Baker-Finch was six under par after only six holes with birdies at the first and second, two more at the fourth and sixth, and in between an eagle-three at the fifth where he was home with a drive and four wood before sinking a putt of some 5 yards. With a two at the eighth Baker-Finch, too, was out in 29 and then went to nine under par for the round with threes at the tenth and twelfth. Again there was the spectre of a 59, but just as the closing holes were the less rewarding for Broadhurst, so they were for this most modest and gentle of Australians. Indeed Baker-Finch, thinking now of the record, did not even match Broadhurst's 63. His bold four wood second was not quite enough to the seventeenth and rolled back into the little gully from where he took three more to get down for a five.

'It was like the days of old on the putting green,' said Baker-Finch. He had decided, after watching Faldo and Norman on television on Friday, that he was playing much too conservatively and resolved to go for everything. He believes he is not only a much more experienced player than he was in 1984, when he was after all only twenty-three, but a much better one now. A victory in America, where he is now on the tour, confirms that, and his whole year was geared to his thoughts of St Andrews. 'All I wanted was to come here and get into contention for the last round,' he said, 'and now I have done it.' Concentration and the determination not to take any shot for granted were just two of his allies.

So they are with Faldo who, in T-shirt and jeans, could be found on the practice green with his coach David Leadbetter, as early as 9.30 a.m., almost six hours before he was due to play. Of course, he was probably not allowed to stay in bed, not when he has two children as young as Natalie and Matthew.

Nevertheless, his putting was the key to his game, allied of course to some more sumptuous iron play. There were, I believe, two moments when he stamped himself as potentially the champion, each in their way breaking the resistance of Norman or at least informing him that here was a golfer who was going to give absolutely nothing away.

At the first hole both pitched beyond the flag and on much the same line, Faldo to 18 feet, Norman perhaps a yard nearer. It was, therefore, Faldo who had to putt first and he holed it, putting the pressure immediately on his opponent, who missed. Psychologically that can have a damaging effect and immediately Norman fell further behind with three

putts at the second. Certainly he got one back at the fourth, birdies were exchanged at the next two holes but there was a two-stroke swing at the ninth, where Faldo had a birdie and Norman three-putted again.

Out in 33 against 36, Faldo was then three strokes ahead and it became four when at the eleventh he hit an eight iron downwind to 15 feet and in the putt went again. But it was the twelfth that somehow told the difference between them. Faldo, with the honour, hit almost his only errant drive of the week deep into the gorse and it was very nearly unplayable. From there he could only chip out sideways but with a brilliant sand wedge to the little shelf on which the flag was perched, he got his third to 8 feet and in went the putt.

At the same hole, Norman wasted two chances, first by driving into a bunker and then, after coming out well, taking three putts from the front of the green. Now in total disarray, Norman drove into a bunker at the thirteenth, and lost further shots at the fifteenth and sixteenth as putt after putt unerringly missed the hole on the left. Faldo, on the other hand, went remorselessly on with another birdie at the sixteenth, his one dropped shot at the seventeenth, but no doubts at all about his finish as he pitched at the last to 2 feet before stroking in his sixth birdie of the round.

'I just have to keep it going for one more day,' said Faldo. 'I have to stay in the same mode, play aggressively and keep going for it. Tomorrow I will not be content to take pars. I want birdies.' Poor Norman. All he wanted was to dig a hole in the ground for himself, though Faldo did say that he had handled his disappointments very well.

Instead it was Payne Stewart, one of America's most consistent players, who was in contention. He did not drop a shot in his 68, though it might conceivably have been one better, since he drove the green at the tenth, which most were doing, but then took three putts. A couple of others, at the first and sixth, were good chances missed from 10 feet or less, but against that he did two putt the thirteenth from 30 yards or more, and that was a bonus.

Stewart acknowledged that he would have to 'shoot a low number' now if he was going to

A huge gallery followed in expectation of a great Faldo v Norman match, but Faldo dominated, stretching his margin to nine strokes with a birdie at the sixteenth after saving par from the gorse at the twelfth. When they shook hands on the last hole, Faldo had a 67 for a record 199 aggregate and Norman, a 76 to be on 208.

have any sort of chance. He knew only too well how strongly Faldo was playing, so well in fact, that 'he just does not make many mistakes.' Not that Stewart made any himself with an outward half of 33 but only one birdie coming home, a three at the last.

Meanwhile, the challenge of Ian Woosnam, which had begun to fade towards the end of his second round, revived with an outward half of 32 but subsided again as he struggled home in 38 for a 70. It was, he said, his driving that let him down because he could not get into the right position on the fairway, perhaps trying to guide the ball rather than just hitting it.

The ball indeed was now very much in Faldo's court and no one, it seemed, now that Norman had slipped out of contention, was better equipped for keeping it there.

(Opposite page) There was a blaze alongside the second hole (above) after Paul Broadhurst (below) had lit a fire of his own with a 63.

Among those in pursuit of Faldo were (clockwise from top left): Craig Parry, Ian Baker-Finch, Ian Woosnam and Frank Nobilo.

Colourful Payne Stewart, with his third successive 68, replaced Norman as a challenger to Faldo on 204.

The Princess Royal visited the Open Championship on the Saturday in her capacity as President of the British Knitting and Export Council. Watching the golf with her were R&A captain Michael Attenborough (bottom left) and Graeme Simmers, chairman of the Championship Committee.

THIRD ROUND RESULTS

HOLE	1	2	3	4	5	6	7	8	9	10	11	12	13	14	15	16	17	18	
PAR	4	4	4	4	5	4	4	3	4	4	3	4	4	5	4	4	4	4	TOTAL
Nick Faldo	3	4	4	4	4	4	4	3	3	4	2	4	4	5	4	3	5	3	67-199
Ian Baker-Finch	3	3	4	3	3	3	4	2	4	3	3	3	4	5	4	4	5	4	64-204
Payne Stewart	4	3	4	4	4	4	3	3	4	4	3	4	4	5	4	4	4	3	68-204
Craig Parry	4	3	4	4	4	4	4	2	4	4	3	4	4	5	3	4	5	4	69-205
Paul Broadhurst	3	4	3	4	4	3	3	2	3	3	3	4	4	5	4	4	4	3	63-206
Frank Nobilo	4	3	4	4	4	3	4	3	4	3	3	4	5	4	4	3	5	4	68-207
Ian Woosnam	3	4	3	4	5	4	3	2	4	5	3	4	4	5	4	4	5	4	70-207
Corey Pavin	3	4	4	4	5	4	3	3	4	4	3	3	4	5	4	4	4	3	68-208
Tim Simpson	3	3	4	4	4	4	5	3	4	3	3	3	5	5	4	4	5	3	69-208
Vicente Fernandez	3	4	4	4	4	4	4	3	4	5	2	3	5	5	4	4	4	3	69-208
Peter Jacobsen	3	4	4	3	4	4	3	5	3	4	4	3	4	5	5	4	3	5	4	70-208
Nick Price	4	4	4	4	5	4	4	3	4	3	3	4	4	5	4	4	5	3	71-208
Greg Norman	4	5	4	3	5	3	4	3	5	4	3	5	5	5	5	5	4	4	76-208

HOLE SUMMARY

HOLE	PAR	EAGLES	BIRDIES	PARS	BOGEYS	HIGHER	RANK	AVERAGE
1	4	0	28	42	2	0	17	3.64
2	4	0	15	48	8	1	10	3.93
3	4	0	11	59	2	0	11	3.88
4	4	0	6	51	14	1	3	4.14
5	5	3	37	27	5	0	18	4.47
6	4	0	13	48	10	1	6	4.00
7	4	0	21	41	10	0	13	3.85
8	3	0	12	55	5	0	12	2.90
9	4	0	18	50	4	0	15	3.81
OUT	36	3	161	421	60	3		34.62
10	4	0	20	47	5	0	16	3.79
11	3	0	9	57	6	0	8	2.96
12	4	0	17	42	13	0	9	3.94
13	4	0	5	47	18	2	2	4.24
14	5	0	10	48	12	2	4	5.11
15	4	0	10	50	12	0	5	4.03
16	4	0	14	47	9	2	6	4.00
17	4	0	2	30	30	10	1	4.68
18	4	0	18	47	7	0	13	3.85
IN	36	0	105	415	112	16		36.60
TOTAL	72	3	266	836	172	19		71.22

1985 champion Sandy Lyle demonstrated a return to form with his 67 in the third round.

Players Below Par	39
Players At Par	10
Players Above Par	23

LOW SCORES

Low First Nine	Ian Baker-Finch	29
	Paul Broadhurst	29
Low Second Nine	Paul Azinger	33
	David Graham	33
	Jeff Sluman	33
Low Round	Paul Broadhurst	63

Mark McNulty was eager to do well in his first tournament at St Andrews.

SUCCESS IS RELATIVE FOR THE CONTENDERS

BY RENTON LAIDLAW

When Mark McNulty stepped up to receive his cheque for a share of second place in the 1990 Open Championship with Payne Stewart, he had every reason to be grateful to a friend who plays golf at Wentworth near London.

Before the French Open, four weeks earlier, McNulty had been looking for a putter with which he could once again hole putts with his now-accustomed flair. His tried-and-trusted Zebra was just not working well enough and he felt it would benefit from a rest. Rummaging through Bernard Gallacher's shop at Wentworth, near his home, McNulty tried this putter and that. None had that extra special feel he knew he needed to make it work for him, until he stumbled across La Femme — a shorter-shafted ladies' putter.

McNulty liked the feel of the club, which had a shaft two and a half inches shorter than a normal club, and suggested to Gallacher that it would fit the bill rather well. Gallacher disagreed, pointing out that the club belonged to a Wentworth member. Further discussion followed, and when McNulty learned to whom the club belonged, he was delighted. He knew him, was sure he would not mind loaning him the club, and was off clutching La Femme quicker than a downhill putt takes off at Augusta.

At the French Open at Chantilly near Paris, McNulty, having practised with the new putter and his old one, left both in his bag on the second day, and incurred a two-shot penalty for his forgetfulness. Walking down the first fairway, he discovered he had one club too many in his bag and knew he had to decide which putter to keep and use. He chose La Femme and went on to shoot a 63, which became a 65 with the penalty. That week he finished fourth and the following week, still putting well, he was sixth in Monte Carlo. At Gleneagles, in the Scottish Open, he came second to runaway winner Ian Woosnam, and when he used the putter for a crucial closing 65 at St Andrews, it meant he had won £135,000 in prize-money in just four weeks. For the time being, the Wentworth member will have to play on without La Femme.

Curiously, McNulty had never played a tournament at St Andrews, far less an Open Championship, so it was with considerable anticipation that he had driven to St Andrews following the Scottish Open. He was playing well, but wondered how he would cope with the special atmosphere at St Andrews, where it is impossible not to be aware of the ghosts of the great golfers who have played there over the years. There was a special reason, too, why McNulty wanted to do well. He has Scottish blood in him. His grandfather had come from Ayr, and had often expressed the wish that Mark might one day win an Open, preferably at St Andrews. That was his dream before he died of cancer in the mid-seventies. Now it was McNulty's hope, as he prepared for the championship which belongs to the world, the major which licks all others for tradition and history.

His practice had gone well. Having rested on the Sunday when heavy rain cut short everyone's preparation, he went with Player on the Monday; David Frost, Nick Price and Ken Trimble from Australia on the Tuesday; and played his final round on Wednesday with Ronan Rafferty. Each day he played very early, and he enjoyed the challenge that the course presented more and more. He felt even more comfortable about his chances after his tune-up with his coach, David Leadbetter, who had found little in his swing that needed to be changed, although that was hardly surprising, with McNulty having had fourteen top-ten finishes in seventeen tournament appearances worldwide in 1990.

McNulty teed up with Andy North and Eamonn Darcy on the first day at what he considered the ideal time, just after 9 a.m., and shot a 74. He played better than that, but was out of bounds, ran up a seven at the long fourteenth and went into the bunker that guards the seventeenth green, taking a five there — a good five because he had been right up against the steep bunker face. He was disappointed at being immediately eight strokes off the lead.

He did better on the second day with a 68, coming alive after three-putting the seventh green. He strung together three birdies in a row from the ninth, birdied the fifteenth and finished the day with a thirty-six hole total of 142, but now he was ten strokes behind the joint leaders, Greg Norman and Nick Faldo. There was no indication as yet that McNulty was about to produce his best performance in an Open.

On the third day, when Norman's challenge disappeared with a forgettable 76 and Faldo took a firm grip on the proceedings, McNulty stayed in touch with another 68, improving his position on the leaderboard, although slipping eleven strokes behind Faldo.

The Zimbabwean, who had begun two of the previous three rounds with a birdie-three, began his last round with a birdie, beat par at the third and although he three-putted from long range at the par-five fifth, he remained cool, calm and composed. Patience is always a key to success at St Andrews. By the ninth he had moved to nine under par, holed from 30 feet at the tenth for a birdie and recovered well from behind the green at the short eleventh to keep the momentum going.

When a 7-footer went in at the twelfth for a birdie and he pitched from 64 yards to 6 feet at the fourteenth, and to just a few inches at the fifteenth for two more sub-par figures, McNulty knew he could make third place. He made par at the sixteenth, but the seventeenth hole would cause him some consternation. His three-iron second shot leaked on the wind and the ball disappeared over the back of the green.

'I remember saying to my caddie, Paul Stevens, that I hoped the ball had finished not on the path

or the road, but on the thin strip of grass between them,' said McNulty. 'I was unlucky. It was right in the middle of the road. In practice Ronan Rafferty had suggested I practice a shot from the road, but I had declined to do so. Now at the seventy-first hole I was faced with the problem shot.'

Yet McNulty could not believe his eyes when he got up to the ball. Somehow, it was sitting, cute as you like, on the top of three small stones. It was teed up so well that he could nip it off the tarmac with his wedge. He was faced with an 18-foot putt for par and admits he did not lift his head until the putt, dead on line, was two inches from the cup and about to drop. He made four there, and again at the last where his tee shot, aimed sensibly on the clock of the R&A Clubhouse, had ended on another road, Granny Clark's Wynd, which is an extension across the eighteenth and first fairways.

The 65 gave him a thirteen-under-par total of 275 and, he thought, third place behind Faldo and Stewart. Before he headed back to the Old Course Hotel to freshen up, he inquired of R&A secretary, Michael Bonallack, whether he was needed at the presentation ceremony. Bonallack said that if he was third on his own, he would be required, but if tied third, they would go with the first two players only. McNulty headed back to his room to await developments.

With Jodie Mudd taking a six at the seventeenth and Payne Stewart dropping a shot at the fourteenth, it was to be expected that Bonallack would call McNulty's room and ask him to come back. McNulty slipped on the course and followed Faldo and Stewart, who had dropped another stroke at the seventeenth and was now just a shot ahead of him on the leaderboard.

A Scottish policeman looked after McNulty as the crowds surged forward, but it was not until he was standing outside the R&A Clubhouse and play had finished that he realized he had done better than he could have hoped for. He had not seen Stewart miss a short par putt on the last hole, which dropped him back to thirteen under par, tied with him. It was the end for McNulty of a perfect week ... well, almost perfect. Only Faldo had prevented him from realizing his grandfather's dream – but then, on the week, Faldo was magnificently unbeatable.

If McNulty ended the championship on a high note, Stewart was less than pleased with his finish. Dropping shots at three of the last six holes not only cost him second place on his own but eased the pressure on Faldo, whom he had battled with all day, having taken over the main challenging role from Norman.

As usual, Stewart had prepared well for the Open, in which he had finished second equal, in 1985, to Sandy Lyle. His acclimatization had included playing the Scottish Open the week before at what he described as gorgeous Gleneagles. 'Three years ago I did not realize such a place existed,' he said.

Stewart had every reason for believing that he would do well in the Open. He was playing solidly and, after visiting his sports psychologist, was getting less annoyed with himself when he did hit the odd poor shot. Since the Masters in April, he had won twice on the US tour and been runner-up twice, and his Open record was good. After missing the cut in 1984, the last time the championship had been played at St Andrews, he had four top-eight finishes. He was one American who had learned quickly how to cope with the humps and hollows of British links golf and, more importantly, enjoyed it. He played the week low-key. Staying privately, he wandered down from his 'digs' each day and did not use the R&A Clubhouse.

He may have been unmissable on the course with his colourful National Football League outfits. Those outfits caused considerable chat among the galleries, especially among the more sedate Scottish supporters. Stewart was aware of so many negative comments about his golfing apparel that he was prompted, at one stage, to point out that what he wore hardly affected the way he played. He was playing well in the colours of the Washington Redskins, Green Bay Packers, New England Patriots and, on the final day, in a Stars and Stripes number he described as the NFL shield. This, in particular, prompted some ribald comments from some, which indicated they questioned the marriage of American football and the R&A game.

Stewart took it all in good heart. He knew, after all, that nobody at St Andrews queried Stewart's considerable golfing talent. Shrewd British fans can spot a quality player a mile off, and they appreciated his talent as he fired three 68s in a row – and found himself five behind. His only hope was that he was saving the best for the last round. He needed something special to have any chance of catching Faldo. It was not to be.

Although Stewart had considered, before the start, that twelve under par might have been good enough to win, and in fact he shot thirteen under, it was only good for a share of second with McNulty. He could not have counted on Faldo's fabulous form. He had made a lot of friends, had handled himself, his game and the Old Course superbly, but had not won. Annoyed enough with himself at the end to decline an invitation to visit the press room, Stewart left St Andrews even more determined to come back and win the Open one day.

So McNulty and Stewart finished five strokes off the pace and one clear of Ian Woosnam, who is still chasing that elusive first major, and Jodie Mudd, the slim American who twice shot 66 during the week. Australians, Greg Norman and Ian Baker-Finch, were tied for sixth, seven strokes behind. For both, that was a disappointment.

Norman had promised so much with his two opening rounds of 66, only to see his challenge crumble when he played with Faldo on the third day and shot 76 to Faldo's 67. As always, Norman was a gracious loser, a role fate has cast him in far too often. Golf is a cruel game. Watching Norman over the first two days, striding along, putting superbly, looking every inch a winner, contrasted sharply with the way it all went wrong for him on the third day – the day that Baker-Finch, who had led with a round to go in 1984 at St Andrews, turned in a 64 – twelve strokes better than Norman.

There was no stopping Nick Faldo, who started and finished with a five-stroke advantage.

DAY

4

FALDO MAINTAINS
TOTAL CONTROL

BY MICHAEL WILLIAMS

It was in the last round of the 1983 Open Championship at Royal Birkdale that Nick Faldo first began to realize that he did not have the swing that would stand up to winning major championships. He had gone out in 33 to lead the field but the 40 strokes he took to come home relegated him to a share of eighth place, five behind Tom Watson.

For someone who had already won three British PGA Championships and that year alone five tournaments, three of them in a row, it was a salutary experience. By the end of 1984 Faldo decided that something had to be done about his swing. It was during the Million Dollar tournament at Sun City, when he finished second to Severiano Ballesteros, that Faldo met for the first time David Leadbetter, who was to re-shape not only his game but his whole career.

By then Nick Price and Denis Watson, two of Leadbetter's other pupils, had in quick succession won the World Series, and Leadbetter's reputation was growing. Faldo and Leadbetter met again at Muirfield Village during the Memorial Tournament the following spring and, not to put too fine a point on it, they went right back to basics and started all over again.

Faldo was under no illusions. He knew it would take two years, and these were two years when he took a lot of criticism for abandoning a method that had, by most standards, served him well enough. But Faldo's standards are not the standards of others. He knew what he wanted and that was to be the best. And he could only be the best if he knew he could stand on the eighteenth fairway on the last day of an Open Championship with a long iron in his hand and know he could hit the green.

The proof and the reward came at Muirfield in the 1987 Open, needing, he knew, a four for his eight-

eenth consecutive par and a possible victory (possible because much depended on what Paul Azinger did behind him). The shot Faldo hit with a five iron made all the toil, sweat and even tears worthwhile. I have with me still the notes I made when he spoke of what he had been going through.

'I was so nervous,' he said, 'because over those last five or six holes I had known I simply dare not make a mistake. If I did, all would be lost. And then comes this vital shot and you can't think about it. You have to hit it from memory. Then I had and it was straight on the flag and I just wanted to shout out "Cor, look at that!" In a way it was like driving a car when you have nearly had an accident. I went hot and cold all at the same time and then it was all over.'

Nor was this the last time Faldo went hot and cold all over. He must have done so too in 1989 when, now with a three iron in his hand, he sent a peerless stroke through the gathering gloom and damp of an Augusta April evening to the eleventh green and sank the putt which won him his first Masters, beating Scott Hoch in a play-off. A year later, only a few months before this St Andrews Open, there was the eight iron, same place, same hole as he made the most of the second shot Raymond Floyd had already deposited in the water, to clinch his second green jacket.

Faldo probably went hot and cold all over at Medinah the previous month, when at the eighteenth he hit a four iron second shot to 8 feet and had the chance of a birdie putt to tie the US Open. In this instance the putt did not go in and the dream of a Grand Slam died. If anything, this only redoubled Faldo's determination to win the Open at St Andrews and here he was, on that final day, waking up to a five-stroke lead in the knowledge that only one man could beat him and that was himself.

As on the Saturday, he rose early and by 9.30 a.m. was on the practice ground with Leadbetter at his side, giving him the once over, or what Faldo likes to describe as a last bit of 'fine tuning'. By midmorning he was back in the Old Course Hotel and asleep. It was, however, not a deep sleep, for Faldo admitted to being 'all knotted up inside', it being such a different feeling to lead when in all his three other majors he had come from behind. 'There was much more pressure,' he confessed.

By 2.30 p.m. he was on the practice green in the shadow of the stand that flanks the first fairway of the Old Course working on his putting stroke. The only other player there was Ian Baker-Finch, with whom he was to play in the last pairing. It was the Australian who seemed the more relaxed, opening the conversation and even drawing a smile from Faldo, who then stopped for a brief chat with Doug Sanders, the man who had come so close to being the champion here twenty years earlier.

As Faldo walked to the tee he looked neither right nor left, other than a quick glance at the clock, before he disappeared into the clubhouse. Baker-Finch followed and they re-emerged together, rivals with a common goal. If it was Faldo's last full shots which had done so much to earn him his one previous Open and his two Masters, it was conversely now his approach to the first green over the Swilcan Burn that emphasized that no one was going to deflect him on this final afternoon.

With a five-stroke lead, it would have been entirely forgivable had he played safely for the middle to back of the green and two-putted. Instead Faldo, after hitting a two iron from the tee, took his sand wedge and pitched in the small area between the burn and the flag, with enough spin on the ball to stop it not a yard away. Birdie. It was an almost outrageously brave shot and he was at once six strokes in front.

As one had known all along, Faldo was not going to lose this one, for he is too good. Nor did he, with a final round of 71, for a total of 270, which is eighteen under par. He finished just as he began this final round, still five strokes ahead of Payne Stewart and also now Mark McNulty, who came belatedly on to the scene with a final round of 65, the lowest of the day. Jodie Mudd, with a flourishing 66, tied fourth with Ian Woosnam (69). Baker-Finch faltered, though not as badly as he had done in 1984. With a 73, he was six strokes better than on that occasion, and came next with Greg Norman, whose 69 hinted only at what might have been had he not taken a 76 in the third round.

Afterwards, Stewart declined to be interviewed and the others were generally resigned to the notion that Faldo was not to be caught on this day or this week. McNulty, a most precise player, had a wonderful round, considering this was the toughest day, the wind quite strong from the east and the flags in the toughest positions of the week. Birdies were not easy, but he had seven. There was also a good effort from Woosnam, and if Europe wanted something more to celebrate, it was worth bearing in mind that three European Tour players were among the top five with Faldo.

If five strokes looks comfortable enough, the day was, nevertheless, not without its uncertainty. At one stage Stewart, bedecked in the Stars and Stripes of the National Football League of America and drawing from my colleague, Raymond Jacobs of the *Glasgow Herald*, the comment that he looked ready for burial at sea, got to within two strokes of his man.

He had made up one stroke by going to the turn in 34 with birdies at the fifth and sixth, Faldo taking 35. He had been in his first bunker of the week at the fourth, coming out beautifully to a green sloping sharply away from him, but not near enough to hole the putt. That was the first shot he had dropped since the seventeenth hole in the first round. However, a huge drive down the fifth and a four iron to the green quickly got the stroke back, and all seemed well.

It was then that Faldo slipped back into one of his more monotonous routines as he made, for once, nothing at all of the loop and it was here that Stewart began to exert some pressure. Though the American did not quite drive the tenth green, he still got down in two, using his putter from the fairway. Then he saved a brilliant par at the eleventh, right over the back of the green with his tee shot but retrieving it with a wonderful pitch back down the slope of the green, from where he holed for a three.

At once, Stewart went four under for the round at the twelfth, and with Faldo static, the difference was only two strokes. As always, it was a tougher route coming home, and Stewart was not up to it. He made the cardinal error of driving neither too left nor straight enough down the thirteenth and was bunkered. He took five. Then at the seventeenth he was too strong with his second shot and took five again. His cause now hopeless, Stewart then became one of the few players all week to fail to get down in two from the Valley of Sin and it all became 37 home for a 71 and no more than a share of second place.

Faldo was well aware of the mishaps that had overtaken Stewart. Two-putt par followed two-putt par for nine successive holes and then at last he got a birdie, a six iron to 8 feet at the sixteenth. For all the cushion he now had, he was in no mood for the spectacular at the seventeenth. He played the hole as a par five, just reaching the front of the putting surface and taking from there three putts, the first time he had done so all week.

'It was smart play,' he argued later. 'Anything can happen at the Road Hole and I would not have liked to have to come to the last green needing two putts to win. I just wanted to walk up the eighteenth and enjoy it, look at the crowd, see the people hanging out of the windows, lap it all up. It is every golfer's dream to win at St Andrews.'

This is something that Ben Hogan never did, and it is him that one sees so much of in Faldo, even though their builds are totally different. Both have sought absolute perfection in the golf swing and neither have allowed themselves to be diverted from that objective. Referring again to Leadbetter, Faldo said, 'We understand the golf swing so well. It is not so much knowing why you hit a bad shot but why you hit a good one that matters. It all goes down in the memory bank and hardly a day goes by when I do not write down my swing thoughts.'

Reflecting on his four major championships, now only one behind the five of Ballesteros, who has won three Opens and two Masters, Faldo finds it hard to put any one of them before another. 'They all mean the same to me for different reasons,' he explained. 'Jack Nicklaus said that of his eighteen. I could not understand it at the time, but I do now.'

His record in the major championships is currently without equal. In his last thirteen, beginning with the 1987 Open, he has finished first, twenty-eighth, thirtieth, second, third, fifth, first, eighteenth, eleventh, ninth, first, third and first. That is the stuff of Jack Nicklaus in his prime.

Reflecting on his performance, Faldo said that he thought the key to his victory was his iron play, though at the same time his putting all week was fabulous. 'When my lead was down to two strokes, it was pretty scary,' he admitted. 'Anything could have happened. There are so many deep bunkers and if I had stuck it in one of those and run up a score, I would have been in serious trouble.'

Faldo had won just as Nicklaus had in the past been expected to win. There were those who were to argue afterwards that there was very little way he could have lost, so difficult were the pin positions on the last day. It made it a golf course that was more difficult to attack than defend and, consequently, it was not surprising that Stewart failed in the end to close the gap between them.

However, the counter to all that was that McNulty managed a 65 and a low score was, therefore, possible. At the same time the Zimbabwean had less to lose, for he had been eleven strokes back with not the slightest chance of winning. He was off to a flier with two birdies in the first three holes and with another at the seventh was out in 33. Two more followed at the tenth and twelfth and then came a delicate sand wedge to the fourteenth, a six iron even closer to the flag at the fifteenth, and there were his seven birdies.

However, there was no doubt that the best player had won, Faldo now assuming the sort of dominance Nicklaus had mentioned earlier in the week when players used to turn their heads in the locker room, look across and say to themselves: 'That is the man we have got to beat.'

Faldo once put it another way. His dream is for people one day to say to one another when talking of the great golfers: 'Yes, but did you ever see Nick Faldo play?' Well, we were lucky enough to see him play this week and that is something none of us who were there will forget.

The town and television cranes in the background, Payne Stewart plays on in pursuit of Faldo.

Robert Gamez (below) was joint twelfth. Putting frustrations got to Sam Torrance (right) who was joint thirty-ninth. Jose Maria Olazabal (below left) and David Graham, here with R&A member Blake Clark, were joint sixteenth and eighth respectively.

Payne Stewart (left) played the fourth round in Stars and Stripes attire, and placed joint second. Fellow Americans Corey Pavin (top) and Donnie Hammond (bottom left) were joint eighth, and Jodie Mudd (bottom right) was joint fourth.

FOURTH ROUND RESULTS

HOLE	1	2	3	4	5	6	7	8	9	10	11	12	13	14	15	16	17	18	
PAR	4	4	4	4	5	4	4	3	4	4	3	4	4	5	4	4	4	4	TOTAL
Nick Faldo	3	4	4	5	4	4	4	3	4	4	3	4	4	5	3	4	5	4	71-270
Mark McNulty	3	4	3	4	5	4	3	3	4	3	3	3	4	4	3	4	4	4	65-275
Payne Stewart	4	4	4	4	4	3	4	3	4	3	3	3	5	5	4	4	5	5	71-275
Jodie Mudd	3	4	4	5	5	4	3	2	4	3	2	3	4	4	3	4	6	3	66-276
Ian Woosnam	3	5	4	4	4	4	3	3	3	3	2	4	4	6	4	4	5	4	69-276
Greg Norman	4	4	5	4	5	4	3	3	4	3	3	4	4	4	3	4	5	3	69-277
Ian Baker-Finch	4	3	4	5	4	4	4	3	4	4	3	4	4	5	4	5	5	4	73-277
David Graham	3	3	4	4	4	4	4	3	4	3	4	3	4	4	5	3	4	3	66-279
Steve Pate	4	5	4	4	4	4	3	2	3	3	3	4	4	5	4	4	5	4	69-279
Donnie Hammond	3	4	4	4	3	4	4	4	4	3	3	4	5	5	3	4	5	4	70-279
Corey Pavin	3	3	4	4	5	3	4	3	4	4	4	4	3	5	4	6	4	4	71-279

HOLE SUMMARY

HOLE	PAR	EAGLES	BIRDIES	PARS	BOGEYS	HIGHER	RANK	AVERAGE
1	4	0	25	37	8	2	15	3.82
2	4	0	9	46	17	0	5	4.11
3	4	0	14	55	3	0	14	3.85
4	4	0	6	47	19	0	3	4.18
5	5	3	32	34	2	1	18	4.53
6	4	0	10	46	16	0	6	4.08
7	4	0	21	44	7	0	16	3.81
8	3	0	10	58	4	0	13	2.92
9	4	0	12	52	8	0	12	3.94
OUT	36	3	139	419	84	3		35.24
10	4	0	25	37	10	0	17	3.79
11	3	1	10	49	11	1	8	3.01
12	4	1	7	50	13	1	6	4.08
13	4	0	4	39	29	0	2	4.35
14	5	0	14	45	11	2	9	5.01
15	4	0	12	50	10	0	10	3.97
16	4	0	9	45	17	1	4	4.14
17	4	0	0	29	36	7	1	4.74
18	4	0	13	49	10	0	11	3.96
IN	36	2	94	393	147	12		37.05
TOTAL	72	5	233	812	231	15		72.29

Players Below Par	26		
Players At Par	13		
Players Above Par	33		

LOW SCORES

Low First Nine	Bernhard Langer	31
Low Second Nine	Mark McNulty	32
	Jodie Mudd	32
	Naomichi Ozaki	32
Low Round	Mark McNulty	65

CHAMPIONSHIP HOLE SUMMARY

HOLE	PAR	EAGLES	BIRDIES	PARS	BOGEYS	HIGHER	RANK	AVERAGE
1	4	1	134	276	38	7	15	3.82
2	4	0	66	290	89	11	4	4.10
3	4	1	108	323	23	1	16	3.81
4	4	0	34	305	112	5	3	4.19
5	5	13	189	220	32	2	18	4.61
6	4	0	68	316	66	6	7	4.03
7	4	0	92	292	69	3	11	3.96
8	3	0	49	364	42	1	9	2.99
9	4	1	102	319	32	2	14	3.85
OUT	36	16	842	2705	503	38		35.36
10	4	1	138	281	36	0	17	3.77
11	3	1	54	332	64	5	5	3.04
12	4	2	83	308	60	3	12	3.95
13	4	0	23	288	131	14	2	4.30
14	5	2	109	264	67	14	10	4.97
15	4	0	59	342	53	2	8	4.00
16	4	0	69	304	77	6	6	4.05
17	4	0	15	197	194	50	1	4.65
18	4	1	98	322	35	0	13	3.86
IN	36	7	648	2638	717	94		36.59
TOTAL	72	23	1490	5343	1220	132		71.95

	FIRST ROUND	SECOND ROUND	THIRD ROUND	FOURTH ROUND	TOTAL
Players Below Par	50	86	39	26	201
Players At Par	30	17	10	13	70
Players Above Par	76	53	23	33	185

ATTENDANCE

PRACTICE ROUNDS	40,546
FIRST ROUND	36,872
SECOND ROUND	42,626
THIRD ROUND	45,587
FOURTH ROUND	43,049
TOTAL	208,680

Nick Faldo says, 'You play the majors for the trophies, the prestige and a place in the record books.'

COMMENTARY

WHY FALDO HAD TO WIN

BY JOHN HOPKINS

The true measure of Nick Faldo's stature in golf was never better demonstrated than when he led the Open Championship by five strokes after Saturday. At the moment there was only one way for him to go. He had *to win*.

Or did he? Let me be argumentative for a moment and suggest that in the grand scheme of things it would not have been the end of the world if Faldo had not won. He still had his wealth, which is sufficient to make him Britain's richest sportsman, and he still had his health.

Best of all, he still had his family. One of the sights of St Andrews that sticks in the mind's eye is of him, within minutes of completing a round, swinging his daughter, Natalie, up on to his shoulders and down again, in short behaving like any normal, child-smitten Dad.

And in case all this was not enough, Faldo didn't have a lot to prove. He had won three of the game's four annual major championships since June 1987 and, in that time, had become the most consistent player in the world in major events, which is as good as saying he was the best player in the world. At age thirty-three, he would have plenty more opportunities.

Such attributes, priceless as they are, were of little consolation to Faldo on Saturday night. He is interested only in victory in the major championships and plans his annual assaults on each of them as a general plans his battle campaigns. 'You play the tour events for the prize money,' he once explained. 'You play the majors for the trophies, the prestige and a place in the record books. I'm not saying I don't play to win prize money. I'm saying I want my name to be recognized in the world of golf. I want people to say that they saw me play.'

No, there were no two ways about it. Faldo had to convert the nest egg of his five-stroke lead into the handsome dividend of his fourth victory in a major. He mustn't fail, not so soon after he missed clawing his way into a play-off for the US Open by one stroke.

For Faldo, starting the last round of the 119th Open was another moment like the play-offs at Augusta in 1989 and 1990 – moments for which he had spent years remodelling his swing and turning himself into the best golfer in the world in a crisis. At such moments he seems to set his shoulders in a way that suggests he isn't going to yield, no matter what. Imagine it in terms of a race, and Faldo and one opponent are shoulder to shoulder entering the last lap. Faldo always gives me the feeling that he will win – and, more to the point, he gives his rival that same feeling.

'No one will catch him if he plays as well as he has done for the first three days,' said Payne Stewart, who lay in joint second place with one round remaining.

Sure enough, no one did. Faldo continued playing as remorselessly as he had on the first three days when he had hardly made a mistake.

On Sunday it was more of the same. He simply never gave anything away. Even when Stewart closed to within two strokes after the twelfth, Faldo knuckled down and, to his relief, noted that the American had fallen back again at the thirteenth by driving into a bunker. A pity. I would have liked to have seen Faldo under pressure for a few more holes. Even he might have begun to sweat a bit then.

As it was, Faldo had a comfortable cushion when he arrived on the sixteenth tee. He was beginning now to dream of victory, yet he knew he daren't make a mistake. 'Take your time,' said his caddie, Fanny Sunneson, as he prepared to drive down the narrow fairway, aiming just left of the Principal's Nose bunkers.

When Faldo is in the groove his swing is enviably

rhythmical, firm, fluid and powerful – and it was now, on the seventeenth tee. He gave this onlooker an impression of controlled power as he drove his ball crisply and watched it fly to its appointed place on the fairway. 'Go on,' he urged it, waving his hand as if trying to make it roll further down the fairway, 'Go on.'

'Nick has very sensibly worked on his rhythm and it's wonderful now,' said a man in a blue blazer and fawn trousers with a Royal and Ancient Golf Club tie. It was none other than Peter Thomson, the wily Australian, who won four events at St Andrews including the Open in 1955, one of his five Open titles. 'Nick's a very good player now and it is his rhythm that is so good.'

'Greg [Norman], on the other hand, is a slugger,' continued Thomson. 'His swing can vary from one round to the next. It can be difficult for him to make it repeat.'

I have watched Faldo in every major championship he has competed in since 1980 and have seen him play outstandingly well at different times on varying continents. There was a courageous back nine in the fourth round of the 1984 US Masters when paired with Ben Crenshaw. He played beautifully for the first nine holes of the fourth round of the Open at Royal Birkdale in 1983 and the opening thirty-six holes of the 1984 US PGA Championship at Shoal Creek.

I have never seen him sustain such a level of excellence as at St Andrews. He had twenty birdies and one eagle in his seventy-two holes. The man who won his first Open with eighteen pars in the fourth round was even steadier over seventy-two holes at St Andrews, where he had forty-seven pars. He bogeyed the Road Hole three times out of the four and had one other bogey – on the fourth on Sunday when he ended in a bunker, his first and last of the week.

In the aftermath of his triumph, Faldo said he had never hit his irons so well. I prefer to remember that his driving was magnificent, which it hadn't been in the US Open at Medinah a month earlier, where time and again he had been forced to use an iron off the tee. (He used his driver fewer than ten times all week.) And his putting was none too shabby, either. He didn't once three-putt in seventy-two holes – his ball wasn't on the putting surface when he used his putter on the seventeenth on Sunday.

Faldo has always been a very good putter. When he was a promising young amateur he used to prac-

David Leadbetter (right) continued to fine-tune Faldo's
game through the Open Championship.

tise on varying surfaces around his parents' home,
first painting some of his mother's nail varnish on
his right thumbnail. If he was to play on a course
with slow greens, he would use the shaggy carpet
in his parents' bedroom; for faster greens he would
practise on the linoleum in the kitchen. Helped by
the fearlessness of youth, he sometimes would hole
almost every putt inside 10 feet in a round.

Starting in 1988 when he had ten second-place
finishes in tournaments around the world, he found
he wasn't holing as many of the 6 to 20-foot putts
as he wanted. He took to practising his putting with
one hand, one of many routines he tried. At the US
Open at Medinah he began using this technique once
again. (He also hit a number of chip shots with his
right hand as well. In part this was done to relieve
the aches he had in his forearms from overworking
earlier in the year.)

On the putting green at Medinah he would put
his left hand in his pocket and use his right hand to
stroke the ball at the target while Sunneson would
crouch behind the hole to see whether the stroke was
correct. At St Andrews it nearly always was.

In sum, he played better than any British golfer
since the days when the austere and efficient Britain
of Queen Victoria burst forth into the colourful era
of the Edwardians and Harry Vardon, J.H. Taylor
and James Braid dominated golf in a way that wasn't
repeated until the age of Palmer, Nicklaus and Player
a half-century later.

The full extent of Faldo's dominance over the
other competitors in the strongest field ever assembled for an Open Championship was never better
demonstrated than in Saturday's third round when
he humiliated Greg Norman, his playing partner.
Faldo's 67 was nine shots better than Norman's and
it may have dimmed for some time, perhaps ever, the
relentless self-confidence of the Australian.

Faldo is so good because he has developed his
own individual strengths to such levels that they
match the strengths of many past champions.

When you watch Faldo at work in his natural
habitat, a golf course, you see a man with the attention to detail of Jack Nicklaus. Faldo knew before
he reached St Andrews that the Road Hole, a tricky

par four, wasn't worth gambling on. It was simply
too dangerous. He decided, therefore, to count it as
a par five and be done with it, a Nicklausian piece
of thinking if ever there was one.

Faldo had enormous determination. On a golf
course or in pursuit of his aims, he appears driv-
en. 'Driven By Women' was the headline put on a
profile I wrote of Faldo before the Open in which I
stressed the Freudian theory that an only son can be
imbued by his mother with such self-confidence that
he doesn't believe he can fail.

Faldo, an only child, received a terrific start in
life from the devotion of his mother, Joyce, who
went to inordinate lengths to provide her son with
what he needed.

Faldo's second wife, Gill, has taken over the
running of Faldo's life just as his mother once did.
And his new caddie, Fanny Sunneson, one of the very
few full-time women caddies on the European Tour,
chivvies, supports and guides Faldo to great effect on
the course.

At heart, Faldo is a quiet and introspective person.
What he needs from a caddie is someone who will lift
his spirits when the dark clouds descend, who will do
the job professionally, who can read his personality
and react accordingly. Sunneson, a cheery Swede,
does all this brilliantly.

Even Faldo's first wife, Melanie, fell into the
same supportive role for a while. I remember writing
a story about Faldo early in 1981 when he was trying
his luck on the US tour.

I wanted to have dinner with Faldo and Melanie
one night and as we walked outside the ropes
watching her husband, I suggested it. 'We could
do it tonight,' Melanie replied. 'Come to our hotel
at 7.30 p.m. and we'll go on from there.'

'But don't you think you ought to check with
Nick?' I asked.

'No, no. That'll be all right,' Melanie replied.

Faldo has always been a hard worker, just as
Henry Cotton was. This was what struck David
Leadbetter, the renowned teacher, when Faldo, then
twenty-eight, went to him and asked to have his
swing rebuilt. 'He was very intense,' Leadbetter said.
'He wanted to be the best. That's what marked him

After Faldo birdied the fifteenth hole (above), only the celebration remained.

out. He was a perfectionist. He was willing to stand by what I said and go ahead and do it no matter what the consequences were. To me that meant he had guts.'

There's no doubt Faldo had guts because few golfers have ever undertaken such drastic reconstruction of their swings at such a comparatively advanced stage of their careers. But this didn't mean he didn't tire of being asked why he had abandoned such an elegant swing, as I once found to my cost. I went to see Faldo at home on the eve of the 1985 Open and as we sat talking in the sitting room I pushed and probed him on this subject. Finally he snapped. His face twisted and he snarled at me: 'Don't you start as well.' I realized I'd gone too far and beat a hasty retreat, covering my tracks with such banalities as 'I'm only playing devil's advocate,' and as I drove home I thought how hard it must be for Faldo to be doing what he was doing.

In those days Faldo's swing was long and loose, Leadbetter recalled. 'On a scale of ten I would rate it at six. It was very handsy.'

The tuning process that was to bring his game to concert pitch for the 1990 Open had begun with a two-hour practice session with Leadbetter after the third round of the Scottish Open the week earlier. That Faldo was getting into the groove became obvious when he went round Gleneagles in 65 the following day.

He followed this encouraging performance with a further session with Leadbetter before they moved across to St Andrews, where Faldo played a few holes on Sunday afternoon while Leadbetter walked alongside. 'If Nick has a weakness it is that he tends to lose his height in his swing,' Leadbetter said. 'He has to watch that he maintains his correct posture so he can keep his swing in the right plane and not lose too much width. But right now Nick's in the mood. He's in the groove,' Leadbetter said.

No assessment of Faldo at this stage of his career is complete without a tribute to the input of Leadbetter, the tall Englishman who grew up in Zimbabwe. He and Faldo are made for one another, the intense, dedicated teacher with a genius for simplifying the complicated, and the intense, dedicated pupil with a voracious appetite for work and a questioning mind.

One of Leadbetter's great strengths is his ability to think up new practice routines for Faldo, which can involve basketballs between the knees or a child's inflatable rubber wings on the arms. One of Faldo's great strengths is that when he is satisfied of the authenticity of Leadbetter's suggestions, he's prepared to go to any lengths to adopt them.

If it's true that without Leadbetter there might be no Faldo as we now know him, then it's also true that without Faldo there might not be any David Leadbetter.

And so with this victory Faldo put himself into the extraordinary position for a Briton of being the favourite for the year's last major championship, the US PGA, both on current form and his past record.

It's possible to speculate that if his putt had gone in instead of clipping the hole and staying out on the seventy-second green of the US Open, Faldo would have won the first three events of the year and would thus be on course for the Grand Slam. Personally, I prefer not to indulge in a game of 'what if' because if Faldo had got into the play-off for the US Open and won, as he probably would, then the pressure might have got to him at St Andrews. It's best to leave the 'ifs' to Rudyard Kipling.

Suffice to say, Faldo's record in major championships since July 1987 would not have disgraced any of the greatest players this century. He has finished: first, twenty-eighth, thirtieth, second, third, fourth, first, eighteenth, eleventh, ninth, first, third, first. It is worthy of comparison with anyone this century save, perhaps, Bobby Jones in his immortal year, 1930. Faldo left St Andrews knowing that at Shoal Creek Country Club in Birmingham, Alabama, he had a chance to equal Ben Hogan's modern record set in 1953 and win three major championships in one season. Not even Jack Nicklaus had done that.

Perhaps that's the greatest tribute one could pay Faldo after his performances in the spring and summer of 1990, namely that he could be about to achieve something that had eluded Nicklaus, the man who had inspired him to take up golf nearly twenty years ago, and the man recently described as the Golfer of the Century.

Actor David Joy portrayed Old Tom Morris during the Open Championship week.

RECORDS OF THE OPEN CHAMPIONSHIP

MOST VICTORIES
6, Harry Vardon, 1896-98-99-1903-11-14
5, James Braid, 1901-05-06-08-10; J.H. Taylor, 1894-95-1900-09-13; Peter Thomson, 1954-55-56-58-65; Tom Watson, 1975-77-80-82-83

MOST TIMES RUNNER-UP OR JOINT RUNNER-UP
7, Jack Nicklaus, 1964-67-68-72-76-77-79
6, J.H. Taylor, 1896-1904-05-06-07-14

OLDEST WINNER
Old Tom Morris, 46 years 99 days, 1867
Roberto de Vicenzo, 44 years 93 days, 1967

YOUNGEST WINNER
Young Tom Morris, 17 years 5 months 8 days, 1868
Willie Auchterlonie, 21 years 24 days, 1893
Severiano Ballesteros, 22 years 3 months 12 days, 1979

YOUNGEST AND OLDEST COMPETITOR
John Ball, 14 years, 1878
Gene Sarazen, 71 years 4 months 13 days, 1973

BIGGEST MARGIN OF VICTORY
13 strokes, Old Tom Morris, 1862
12 strokes, Young Tom Morris, 1870
8 strokes, J.H. Taylor, 1900 and 1913; James Braid, 1908
6 strokes, Bobby Jones, 1927; Walter Hagen, 1929; Arnold Palmer, 1962; Johnny Miller, 1976

LOWEST WINNING AGGREGATES
268 (68, 70, 65, 65), Tom Watson, Turnberry, 1977
270 (67, 65, 67, 71), Nick Faldo, St Andrews, 1990
271 (68, 70, 64, 69), Tom Watson, Muirfield, 1980
273 (67,71, 70, 65), Severiano Ballesteros, Royal Lytham, 1988

LOWEST AGGREGATES BY RUNNER-UP
269 (68, 70, 65, 66), Jack Nicklaus, Turnberry, 1977
275 (68, 67, 71, 69), Lee Trevino, Muirfield, 1980
275 (70, 67, 69, 69), Nick Price, Royal Lytham, 1988
275 (69, 70, 72, 64), Greg Norman, Royal Troon, 1989
275 (68, 67, 69, 71), Wayne Grady, Royal Troon, 1989
275 (74, 68, 68, 65), Mark McNulty, St Andrews, 1990
275 (68, 68, 68, 71), Payne Stewart, St Andrews, 1990

LOWEST AGGREGATE BY AN AMATEUR
283 (74, 70, 71, 68), Guy Wolstenholme, St Andrews, 1960

LOWEST INDIVIDUAL ROUND
63, Mark Hayes, second round, Turnberry, 1977; Isao Aoki, third round, Muirfield, 1980; Greg Norman, second round, Turnberry, 1986; Paul Broadhurst, third round, St Andrews, 1990

LOWEST INDIVIDUAL ROUND BY AN AMATEUR
66, Frank Stranahan, fourth round, Troon, 1950

LOWEST FIRST ROUND
64, Craig Stadler, Royal Birkdale, 1983; Christy O'Connor Jr., Royal St George's, 1985; Rodger Davis, Muirfield, 1987

LOWEST SECOND ROUND
63, Mark Hayes, Turnberry, 1977; Greg Norman, Turnberry, 1986

LOWEST THIRD ROUND
63, Isao Aoki, Muirfield, 1980; Paul Broadhurst, St Andrews, 1990

LOWEST FOURTH ROUND
64, Graham Marsh, Royal Birkdale, 1983; Severiano Ballesteros, Turnberry, 1986; Greg Norman, Royal Troon, 1989

LOWEST FIRST 36 HOLES
132 (67, 65) Henry Cotton, Sandwich, 1934; (66, 66) Greg Norman and (67,65) Nick Faldo, St Andrews, 1990

LOWEST SECOND 36 HOLES
130 (65, 65), Tom Watson, Turnberry, 1977

LOWEST FIRST 54 HOLES
199 (67, 65, 67), Nick Faldo, St Andrews, 1990
202 (68, 70, 64), Tom Watson, Muirfield, 1980

LOWEST FINAL 54 HOLES
200 (70, 65, 65), Tom Watson, Turnberry, 1977

LOWEST 9 HOLES
28, Denis Durnian, first 9, Royal Birkdale, 1983
29, Peter Thomson and Tom Haliburton, first 9, Royal

Lytham, 1958; Tony Jacklin, first 9, St Andrews, 1970; Bill Longmuir, first 9, Royal Lytham, 1979; David J. Russell, first 9, Royal Lytham, 1988; Ian Baker-Finch and Paul Broadhurst, first 9, St Andrews, 1990

CHAMPIONS IN THREE DECADES
Harry Vardon, 1896, 1903, 1911
J.H. Taylor, 1894, 1900, 1913
Gary Player, 1959, 1968, 1974

BIGGEST SPAN BETWEEN FIRST AND LAST VICTORIES
19 years, J.H. Taylor, 1894-1913
18 years, Harry Vardon, 1896-1914
15 years, Gary Player, 1959-74
14 years, Henry Cotton, 1934-48

SUCCESSIVE VICTORIES
4, Young Tom Morris, 1868-72. No championship in 1871
3, Jamie Anderson, 1877-79; Bob Ferguson, 1880-82, Peter Thomson, 1954-56
2, Old Tom Morris, 1861-62; J.H. Taylor, 1894-95; Harry Vardon, 1898-99; James Braid, 1905-06; Bobby Jones, 1926-27; Walter Hagen, 1928-29; Bobby Locke, 1949-50; Arnold Palmer, 1961-62; Lee Trevino, 1971-72; Tom Watson, 1982-83

VICTORIES BY AMATEURS
3, Bobby Jones, 1926-27-30
2, Harold Hilton, 1892-97
1, John Ball, 1890
Roger Wethered lost a play-off in 1921

HIGHEST NUMBER OF TOP FIVE FINISHES
16, J.H. Taylor and Jack Nicklaus
15, Harry Vardon and James Braid

HIGHEST NUMBER OF ROUNDS UNDER 70
29, Jack Nicklaus
21, Tom Watson
19, Lee Trevino, Nick Faldo
15, Peter Thomson
14, Severiano Ballesteros
13, Gary Player, Ben Crenshaw
12, Bobby Locke, Arnold Palmer, Bernhard Langer
10, Greg Norman, Payne Stewart

OUTRIGHT LEADER AFTER EVERY ROUND
Willie Auchterlonie, 1893; J.H. Taylor, 1894 and 1900; James Braid, 1908; Ted Ray, 1912; Bobby Jones, 1927; Gene Sarazen, 1932; Henry Cotton, 1934; Tom Weiskopf, 1973

RECORD LEADS (SINCE 1892)
After 18 holes:
4 strokes, James Braid, 1908; Bobby Jones, 1927; Henry Cotton, 1934; Christy O'Connor Jr., 1985
After 36 holes:
9 strokes, Henry Cotton, 1934
After 54 holes:
10 strokes, Henry Cotton, 1934
7 strokes, Tony Lema, 1964
6 strokes, James Braid, 1908
5 strokes, Arnold Palmer, 1962; Bill Rogers, 1981;

Nick Faldo, 1990

CHAMPIONS WITH EACH ROUND LOWER THAN PREVIOUS ONE
Jack White, 1904, Sandwich, 80, 75, 72, 69
James Braid, 1906, Muirfield, 77, 76, 74, 73
Ben Hogan, 1953, Carnoustie, 73, 71, 70, 68
Gary Player, 1959, Muirfield, 75, 71, 70, 68

CHAMPION WITH FOUR ROUNDS THE SAME
Densmore Shute, 1933, St Andrews, 73, 73, 73, 73 (excluding the play-off)

BIGGEST VARIATION BETWEEN ROUNDS OF A CHAMPION
14 strokes, Henry Cotton, 1934, second round 65, fourth round 79
11 strokes, Jack White, 1904, first round 80, fourth round 69; Greg Norman, 1986, first round 74, second round 63, third round 74

BIGGEST VARIATION BETWEEN TWO ROUNDS
17 strokes, Jack Nicklaus, 1981, first round 83, second round 66; Ian Baker-Finch, 1986, first round 86, second round 69

BEST COMEBACK BY CHAMPIONS
After 18 holes:
Harry Vardon, 1896, 11 strokes behind the leader
After 36 holes:
George Duncan, 1920, 13 strokes behind the leader
After 54 holes:
Jim Barnes, 1925, 5 strokes behind the leader
Of non-champions, Greg Norman, 1989, 7 strokes behind the leader and lost in a play-off

CHAMPIONS WITH FOUR ROUNDS UNDER 70
None
Arnold Palmer, 1962, Tom Watson, 1977 and 1980, Severiano Ballesteros, 1984, Mark Calcavecchia, 1989, and Nick Faldo, 1990, had three rounds under 70
Of non-champions, Phil Rodgers, 1963, Jack Nicklaus, 1977, Lee Trevino, 1980, Nick Faldo, 1984, Nick Price and Curtis Strange, 1988, Wayne Grady and Tom Watson, 1989, Mark McNulty, Payne Stewart, Ian Woosnam and Greg Norman, 1990, had three rounds under 70

BEST FINISHING ROUND BY A CHAMPION
65, Tom Watson, Turnberry, 1977; Severiano Ballesteros, Royal Lytham, 1988
66, Johnny Miller, Royal Birkdale, 1976

WORST FINISHING ROUND BY A CHAMPION SINCE 1920
79, Henry Cotton, Sandwich, 1934
78, Reg Whitcombe, Sandwich, 1938
77, Walter Hagen, Hoylake, 1924

WORST OPENING ROUND BY A CHAMPION SINCE 1919
80, George Duncan, Deal, 1920 (he also had a second round of 80)
77, Walter Hagen, Hoylake, 1924

BEST OPENING ROUND BY A CHAMPION
66, Peter Thomson, Royal Lytham, 1958
67, Henry Cotton, Sandwich, 1934; Tom Watson, Royal Birkdale, 1983; Severiano Ballesteros, Royal Lytham, 1988; Nick Faldo, St Andrews, 1990

BIGGEST RECOVERY IN 18 HOLES BY A CHAMPION
George Duncan, Deal, 1920, was 13 strokes behind the leader, Abe Mitchell, after 36 holes and level after 54

MOST APPEARANCES ON FINAL DAY (SINCE 1892)
30, J.H. Taylor
28, Jack Nicklaus
27, Harry Vardon, James Braid
26, Peter Thomson
24, Gary Player
23, Dai Rees
22, Henry Cotton

CHAMPIONSHIP WITH HIGHEST NUMBER OF ROUNDS UNDER 70
85, St Andrews, 1990

CHAMPIONSHIP SINCE 1946 WITH THE FEWEST ROUNDS UNDER 70
St Andrews, 1946; Hoylake, 1947; Portrush, 1951; Hoylake, 1956; Carnoustie, 1968. All had only two rounds under 70

LONGEST COURSE
Carnoustie, 1968, 7252 yd (6631 m)

COURSES MOST OFTEN USED
St Andrews and Prestwick (but not since 1925), 24; Muirfield, 13; Sandwich, 11; Hoylake, 10; Royal Lytham, 8; Musselburgh, Royal Birkdale and Royal Troon, 6; Carnoustie, 5; Deal and Turnberry, 2; Royal Portrush and Prince's, 1

PRIZE MONEY

Year	Total	First Prize
1860	nil	nil
1863	10	nil
1864	16	6
1876	20	20
1889	22	8
1891	28.50	10
1892	110	(Amateur winner)
1893	100	30
1910	125	50
1920	225	75
1927	275	100
1930	400	100
1931	500	100
1946	1,000	150
1949	1,700	300
1953	2,450	500
1954	3,500	750
1955	3,750	1,000
1958	4,850	1,000
1959	5,000	1,000
1960	7,000	1,250
1961	8,500	1,400
1963	8,500	1,500
1965	10,000	1,750
1966	15,000	2,100
1968	20,000	3,000
1969	30,000	4,250
1970	40,000	5,250
1971	45,000	5,500
1972	50,000	5,500
1975	75,000	7,500
1977	100,000	10,000
1978	125,000	12,500
1979	155,000	15,500
1980	200,000	25,000
1982	250,000	32,000
1983	300,000	40,000
1984	451,000	55,000
1985	530,000	65,000
1986	600,000	70,000
1987	650,000	75,000
1988	700,000	80,000
1989	750,000	80,000
1990	825,000	85,000

ATTENDANCE

Year	Attendance
1962	37,098
1963	24,585
1964	35,954
1965	32,927
1966	40,182
1967	29,880
1968	51,819
1969	46,001
1970	81,593
1971	70,076
1972	84,746
1973	78,810
1974	92,796
1975	85,258
1976	92,021
1977	87,615
1978	125,271
1979	134,501
1980	131,610
1981	111,987
1982	133,299
1983	142,892
1984	193,126
1985	141,619
1986	134,261
1987	139,189
1988	191,334
1989	160,639
1990	208,680

The former Open champions who came to St Andrews this year joined for a photograph, then dinner together.

PAST RESULTS

*Denotes amateurs

1860 PRESTWICK

Willie Park, Musselburgh	55	59	60	174
Tom Morris Sr, Prestwick	58	59	59	176
Andrew Strath, St Andrews				180
Robert Andrew, Perth				191
George Brown, Blackheath				192
Charles Hunter, Prestwick St Nicholas				195

1861 PRESTWICK

Tom Morris Sr, Prestwick	54	56	53	163
Willie Park, Musselburgh	54	54	59	167
William Dow, Musselburgh	59	58	54	171
David Park, Musselburgh	58	57	57	172
Robert Andrew, Perth	58	61	56	175
Peter McEwan, Bruntsfield	56	60	62	178

1862 PRESTWICK

Tom Morris Sr, Prestwick	52	55	56	163
Willie Park, Musselburgh	59	59	58	176
Charles Hunter, Prestwick	60	60	58	178
William Dow, Musselburgh	60	58	63	181
*James Knight, Prestwick	62	61	63	186
*J.F. Johnston, Prestwick	64	69	75	208

1863 PRESTWICK

Willie Park, Musselburgh	56	54	58	168
Tom Morris Sr, Prestwick	56	58	56	170
David Park, Musselburgh	55	63	54	172
Andrew Strath, St Andrews	61	55	58	174
George Brown, St Andrews	58	61	57	176
Robert Andrew, Perth	62	57	59	178

1864 PRESTWICK

Tom Morris Sr, Prestwick	54	58	55	167
Andrew Strath, St Andrews	56	57	56	169
Robert Andrew, Perth	57	58	60	175
Willie Park, Musselburgh	55	67	55	177
William Dow, Musselburgh	56	58	67	181
William Strath, St Andrews	60	62	60	182

1865 PRESTWICK

Andrew Strath, St Andrews	55	54	53	162
Willie Park, Musselburgh	56	52	56	164
William Dow, Musselburgh				171
Robert Kirk, St Andrews	64	54	55	173
Tom Morris Sr, St Andrews	57	61	56	174
William Doleman, Glasgow	62	57	59	178

1866 PRESTWICK

Willie Park, Musselburgh	54	56	59	169
David Park, Musselburgh	58	57	56	171
Robert Andrew, Perth	58	59	59	176
Tom Morris Sr, St Andrews	61	58	59	178
Robert Kirk, St Andrews	60	62	58	180
Andrew Strath, Prestwick	61	61	60	182
*William Doleman, Glasgow	60	60	62	182

1867 PRESTWICK

Tom Morris, St Andrews	58	54	58	170
Willie Park, Musselburgh	58	56	58	172
Andrew Strath, St Andrews	61	57	56	174
Tom Morris Jr, St Andrews	58	59	58	175
Robert Kirk, St Andrews	57	60	60	177
*William Doleman, Glasgow	55	66	57	178

1868 PRESTWICK

Tom Morris Jr, St Andrews	50	55	52	157
Robert Andrew, Perth	53	54	52	159
Willie Park, Musselburgh	58	50	54	162
Robert Kirk, St Andrews	56	59	56	171
John Allen, Westward Ho!	54	52	63	172
Tom Morris St, St Andrews	56	62	58	176

1869 PRESTWICK

Tom Morris Jr, St Andrews	51	54	49	154
Tom Morris Sr, St Andrews	54	50	53	157
*S. Mure Fergusson, Royal and Ancient	57	54	54	165
Robert Kirk, St Andrews	53	58	57	168
David Strath, St Andrews	53	56	60	169
Jamie Anderson, St Andrews	60	56	57	173

1870 PRESTWICK

Tom Morris Jr, St Andrews	47	51	51	149
Bob Kirk, Royal Blackheath	52	52	57	161
David Strath, St Andrews	54	49	58	161
Tom Morris Sr, St Andrews	56	52	54	162
*William Doleman, Musselburgh	57	56	58	171
Willie Park, Musselburgh	60	55	58	173

1871 NO COMPETITION

1872 PRESTWICK

Tom Morris Jr, St Andrews	57	56	53	166
David Strath, St Andrews	56	52	61	169
*William Doleman, Musselburgh	63	60	54	177
Tom Morris Sr, St Andrews	62	60	57	179
David Park, Musselburgh	61	57	61	179
Charlie Hunter, Prestwick	60	60	69	189

1873 ST ANDREWS

Tom Kidd, St Andrews	91	88	179
Jamie Anderson, St Andrews	91	89	180
Tom Morris Jr, St Andrews	94	89	183
Bob Kirk, Royal Blackheath	91	92	183
David Strath, St Andrews	97	90	187
Walter Gourlay, St Andrews	92	96	188

1874 MUSSELBURGH

Mungo Park, Musselburgh	75	84	159
Tom Morris Jr, St Andrews	83	78	161
George Paxton, Musselburgh	80	82	162
Bob Martin, St Andrews	85	79	164
Jamie Anderson, St Andrews	82	83	165
David Park, Musselburgh	83	83	166
W. Thomson, Edinburgh	84	82	166

1875 PRESTWICK

Willie Park, Musselburgh	56	59	51	166
Bob Martin, St Andrews	56	58	54	168
Mungo Park, Musselburgh	59	57	55	171
Robert Ferguson, Musselburgh	58	56	58	172
James Rennie, St Andrews	61	59	57	177
David Strath, St Andrews	59	61	58	178

1876 ST ANDREWS

Bob Martin, St Andrews	86	90	176
David Strath, North Berwick	86	90	176
(Martin was awarded the title when Strath refused to play-off)			
Willie Park, Musselburgh	94	89	183
Tom Morris Sr, St Andrews	90	95	185
W. Thomson, Elie	90	95	185
Mungo Park, Musselburgh	95	90	185

1877 MUSSELBURGH

Jamie Anderson, St Andrews	40	42	37	41	160
Bob Pringle, Musselburgh	44	38	40	40	162
Bob Ferguson, Musselburgh	40	40	40	44	164
William Cosgrove, Musselburgh	41	39	44	40	164
David Strath, North Berwick	45	40	38	43	166
William Brown, Musselburgh	39	41	45	41	166

1878 PRESTWICK

Jamie Anderson, St Andrews	53	53	51	157
Bob Kirk, St Andrews	53	55	51	159
J.O.F. Morris, St Andrews	50	56	55	161
Bob Martin, St Andrews	57	53	55	165
* John Ball, Hoylake	53	57	55	165
Willie Park, Musselburgh	53	56	57	166
William Cosgrove, Musselburgh	53	56	55	166

1879 ST ANDREWS

Jamie Anderson, St Andrews	84	85	169
James Allan, Westward Ho!	88	84	172
Andrew Kirkaldy, St Andrews	86	86	172
George Paxton, Musselburgh			174
Tom Kidd, St Andrews			175
Bob Ferguson, Musselburgh			176

1880 MUSSELBURGH

Bob Ferguson, Musselburgh	81	81	162
Peter Paxton, Musselburgh	81	86	167
Ned Cosgrove, Musselburgh	82	86	168
George Paxton, Musselburgh	85	84	169
Bob Pringle, Musselburgh	90	79	169
David Brown, Musselburgh	86	83	169

1881 PRESTWICK

Bob Ferguson, Musselburgh	53	60	57	170
Jamie Anderson, St Andrews	57	60	56	173
Ned Cosgrove, Musselburgh	61	59	57	177
Bob Martin, St Andrews	57	62	59	178
Tom Morris Sr, St Andrews	58	65	58	181
Willie Campbell, Musselburgh	60	56	65	181
Willie Park Jr, Musselburgh	66	57	58	181

1882 ST ANDREWS

Bob Ferguson, Musselburgh	83	88	171
Willie Fernie, Dumfries	88	86	174
Jamie Anderson, St Andrews	87	88	175
John Kirkaldy, St Andrews	86	89	175
Bob Martin, St Andrews	89	86	175
* Fitz Boothby, St Andrews	86	89	175

1883 MUSSELBURGH

Willie Fernie, Dumfries	75	84	159
Bob Ferguson, Musselburgh	78	80	159
(Fernie won play-off 158 to 159)			
William Brown, Musselburgh	83	77	160
Bob Pringle, Musselburgh	79	82	161
Willie Campbell, Musselburgh	80	83	163
George Paxton, Musselburgh	80	83	163

1884 PRESTWICK

Jack Simpson, Carnoustie	78	82	160
David Rollan, Elie	81	83	164
Willie Fernie, Felixstowe	80	84	164
Willie Campbell, Musselburgh	84	85	169
Willie Park Jr, Musselburgh	86	83	169
Ben Sayers, North Berwick	83	87	170

1885 ST ANDREWS

Bob Martin, St Andrews	84	87	171
Archie Simpson, Carnoustie	83	89	172
David Ayton, St Andrews	89	84	173
Willie Fernie, Felixstowe	89	85	174
Willie Park Jr, Musselburgh	86	88	174
Bob Simpson, Carnoustie	85	89	174

1886 MUSSELBURGH

David Brown, Musselburgh	79	78	157
Willie Campbell, Musselburgh	78	81	159
Ben Campbell, Musselburgh	79	81	160
Archie Simpson, Carnoustie	82	79	161
Willie Park Jr, Musselburgh	84	77	161
Thomas Gossett, Musselburgh	82	79	161
Bob Ferguson, Musselburgh	82	79	161

1887 PRESTWICK

Willie Park Jr, Musselburgh	82	79	161
Bob Martin, St Andrews	81	81	162
Willie Campbell, Prestwick	77	87	164
* Johnny Laidlay, Honourable Company	86	80	166
Ben Sayers, North Berwick	83	85	168
Archie Simpson, Carnoustie	81	87	168

1888 ST ANDREWS

Jack Burns, Warwick		86	85	171
David Anderson Jr, St Andrews		86	86	172
Ben Sayers, North Berwick		85	87	172
Willie Campbell, Prestwick		84	90	174
* Leslie Balfour, Edinburgh		86	89	175
Andrew Kirkaldy, St Andrews		87	89	176
David Grant, North Berwick		88	88	176

1889 MUSSELBURGH

Willie Park Jr, Musselburgh	39	39	39	38	155
Andrew Kirkaldy, St Andrews	39	38	39	39	155
(Park won play-off 158 to 163)					
Ben Sayes, North Berwick	39	40	41	39	159
* Johnny Laidlay, Honourable Company	42	39	40	41	162
David Brown, Musselburgh	43	39	41	39	162
Willie Fernie, Troon	45	39	40	40	164

1890 PRESTWICK

* John Ball, Royal Liverpool	82	82	164
Willie Fernie, Troon	85	82	167
Archie Simpson, Carnoustie	85	82	167
Willie Park Jr, Musselburgh	90	80	170
Andrew Kirkaldy, St Andrews	81	89	170
* Horace Hutchinson, Royal North Devon	87	85	172

1891 ST ANDREWS

Hugh Kirkaldy, St Andrews	83	83	166
Willie Fernie, Troon	84	84	168
Andrew Kirkaldy, St Andrews	84	84	168
S. Mure Fergusson, Royal and Ancient	86	84	170
W.D. More, Chester	84	87	171
Willie Park Jr, Musselburgh	88	85	173

(From 1892 the competition was extended to 72 holes)

1892 MUIRFIELD

* Harold Hilton, Royal Liverpool	78	81	72	74	305
* John Ball Jr, Royal Liverpool	75	80	74	79	308
James Kirkaldy, St Andrews	77	83	73	75	308
Sandy Herd, Huddersfield	77	78	77	76	308
J. Kay, Seaton Carew	82	78	74	78	312
Ben Sayers, North Berwick	80	76	81	75	312

1893 PRESTWICK

Willie Auchterlonie, St Andrews	78	81	81	82	322
* Johnny Laidlay, Honourable Company	80	83	80	81	324
Sandy Herd, Huddersfield	82	81	78	84	325
Hugh Kirkaldy, St Andrews	83	79	82	82	326
Andrew Kirkaldy, St Andrews	85	82	82	77	326
J. Kay, Seaton Carew	81	81	80	85	327
R. Simpson, Carnoustie	81	81	80	85	327

1894 SANDWICH

J.H. Taylor, Winchester	84	80	81	81	326
Douglas Rolland, Limpsfield	86	79	84	82	331
Andrew Kirkaldy, St Andrews	86	79	83	84	332
A. Toogood, Eltham	84	85	82	82	333
Willie Fernie, Troon	84	84	86	80	334
Harry Vardon, Bury St Edmunds	86	86	82	80	334
Ben Sayers, North Berwick	85	81	84	84	334

1895 ST ANDREWS

J.H. Taylor, Winchester	86	78	80	78	322
Sandy Herd, Huddersfield	82	77	82	85	326
Andrew Kirkaldy, St Andrews	81	83	84	84	332
G. Pulford, Royal Liverpool	84	81	83	87	335
Archie Simpson, Aberdeen	88	85	78	85	336
Willie Fernie, Troon	86	79	86	86	337
David Brown, Malvern	81	89	83	84	337
David Anderson, Panmure	86	83	84	84	337

1896 MUIRFIELD

Harry Vardon, Ganton	83	78	78	77	316
J.H. Taylor, Winchester	77	78	81	80	316
(Vardon won play-off 157 to 161)					
*Freddie G. Tait, Black Watch	83	75	84	77	319
Willie Fernie, Troon	78	79	82	80	319
Sandy Herd, Huddersfield	72	84	79	85	320
James Braid, Romford	83	81	79	80	323

1897 HOYLAKE

*Harold H. Hilton, Royal Liverpool	80	75	84	75	314
James Braid, Romford	80	74	82	79	315
*Freddie G. Tait, Black Watch	79	79	80	79	317
G. Pulford, Royal Liverpool	80	79	79	79	317
Sandy Herd, Huddersfield	78	81	79	80	318
Harry Vardon, Ganton	84	80	80	76	320

1898 PRESTWICK

Harry Vardon, Ganton	79	75	77	76	307
Willie Park, Musselburgh	76	75	78	79	308
*Harold H. Hilton, Royal Liverpool	76	81	77	75	309
J.H. Taylor, Winchester	78	78	77	79	312
*Freddie G. Tait, Black Watch	81	77	75	82	315
D. Kinnell, Leven	80	77	79	80	316

1899 SANDWICH

Harry Vardon, Ganton	76	76	81	77	310
Jack White, Seaford	79	79	82	75	315
Andrew Kirkaldy, St Andrews	81	79	82	77	319
J.H. Taylor, Mid-Surrey	77	76	83	84	320
James Braid, Romford	78	78	83	84	322
Willie Fernie, Troon	79	83	82	78	322

1900 ST ANDREWS

J.H. Taylor, Mid-Surrey	79	77	78	75	309
Harry Vardon, Ganton	79	81	80	78	317
James Braid, Romford	82	81	80	79	322
Jack White, Seaford	80	81	82	80	323

Willie Auchterlonie, St Andrews	81	85	80	80	326
Willie Park Jr, Musselburgh	80	83	81	84	328

1901 MUIRFIELD

James Braid, Romford	79	76	74	80	309
Harry Vardon, Ganton	77	78	79	78	312
J.H. Taylor, Mid-Surrey	79	83	74	77	313
*Harold H. Hilton, Royal Liverpool	89	80	75	76	320
Sandy Herd, Huddersfield	87	81	81	76	325
Jack White, Seaford	82	82	80	82	326

1902 HOYLAKE

Sandy Herd, Huddersfield	77	76	73	81	307
Harry Vardon, South Herts	72	77	80	79	308
James Braid, Walton Heath	78	76	80	74	308
R. Maxwell, Honourable Company	79	77	79	74	309
Tom Vardon, Ilkley	80	76	78	79	313
J.H. Taylor, Mid-Surrey	81	76	77	80	314
D. Kinnell, Leven	78	80	79	77	314
*Harold H. Hilton, Royal Liverpool	79	76	81	78	314

1903 PRESTWICK

Harry Vardon, South Herts	73	77	72	78	300
Tom Vardon, Ilkley	76	81	75	74	306
Jack White, Sunningdale	77	78	74	79	308
Sandy Herd, Huddersfield	73	83	76	77	309
James Braid, Walton Heath	77	79	79	75	310
R. Thompson, North Berwick	83	78	77	76	314
A.H. Scott, Elie	77	77	83	77	314

1904 SANDWICH

Jack White, Sunningdale	80	75	72	69	296
James Braid, Walton Heath	77	80	69	71	297
J.H. Taylor, Mid-Surrey	77	78	74	68	297
Tom Vardon, Ilkley	77	77	75	72	301
Harry Vardon, South Herts	76	73	79	74	302
James Sherlock, Stoke Poges	83	71	78	77	309

1905 ST ANDREWS

James Braid, Walton Heath	81	78	78	81	318
J.H. Taylor, Mid-Surrey	80	85	78	80	323
R. Jones, Wimbledon Park	81	77	87	78	323
J. Kinnell, Purley Downs	82	79	82	81	324
Arnaud Massy, La Boulie	81	80	82	82	325
E. Gray, Littlehampton	82	81	84	78	325

1906 MUIRFIELD

James Braid, Walton Heath	77	76	74	73	300
J.H. Taylor, Mid-Surrey	77	72	75	80	304
Harry Vardon, South Herts	77	73	77	78	305
J. Graham Jr, Royal Liverpool	71	79	78	78	306
R. Jones, Wimbledon Park	74	78	73	83	308
Arnaud Massy, La Boulie	76	80	76	78	310

1907 HOYLAKE

Arnaud Massy, La Boulie	76	81	78	77	312
J.H. Taylor, Mid-Surrey	79	79	76	80	314

Tom Vardon, Sandwich	81	81	80	75	317
G. Pulford, Royal Liverpool	81	78	80	78	317
Ted Ray, Ganton	83	80	79	76	318
James Braid, Walton Heath	82	85	75	76	318

1908 PRESTWICK

James Braid, Walton Heath	70	72	77	72	291
Tom Ball, West Lancashire	76	73	76	74	299
Ted Ray, Ganton	79	71	75	76	301
Sandy Herd, Huddersfield	74	74	79	75	302
Harry Vardon, South Herts	79	78	74	75	306
D. Kinnell, Prestwick St Nicholas	75	73	80	78	306

1909 DEAL

J.H. Taylor, Mid-Surrey	74	73	74	74	295
James Braid, Walton Heath	79	73	73	74	299
Tom Ball, West Lancashire	74	75	76	76	301
C. Johns, Southdown	72	76	79	75	302
T.G. Renouf, Manchester	76	78	76	73	303
Ted Ray, Ganton	77	76	76	75	304

1910 ST ANDREWS

James Braid, Walton Heath	76	73	74	76	299
Sandy Herd, Huddersfield	78	74	75	76	303
George Duncan, Hanger Hill	73	77	71	83	304
Laurie Ayton, Bishops Stortford	78	76	75	77	306
Ted Ray, Ganton	76	77	74	81	308
W. Smith, Mexico	77	71	80	80	308
J. Robson, West Surrey	75	80	77	76	308

1911 SANDWICH

Harry Vardon, South Herts	74	74	75	80	303
Arnaud Massy, St Jean de Luz	75	78	74	76	303
(Play-off; Massy conceded at the 35th hole)					
Harold Hilton, Royal Liverpool	76	74	78	76	304
Sandy Herd, Coombe Hill	77	73	76	78	304
Ted Ray, Ganton	76	72	79	78	305
James Braid, Walton Heath	78	75	74	78	305
J.H. Taylor, Mid-Surrey	72	76	78	79	305

1912 MUIRFIELD

Ted Ray, Oxhey	71	73	76	75	295
Harry Vardon, South Herts	75	72	81	71	299
James Braid, Walton Heath	77	71	77	78	303
George Duncan, Hanger Hill	72	77	78	78	305
Laurie Ayton, Bishops Stortford	74	80	75	79	308
Sandy Herd, Coombe Hill	76	81	76	76	309

1913 HOYLAKE

J.H. Taylor, Mid-Surrey	73	75	77	79	304
Ted Ray, Oxhey	73	74	81	84	312
Harry Vardon, South Herts	79	75	79	80	313
M. Moran, Dollymount	76	74	89	74	313
Johnny J. McDermott, USA	75	80	77	83	315
T.G. Renouf, Manchester	75	78	84	78	315

1914 PRESTWICK

Harry Vardon, South Herts	73	77	78	78	306
J.H. Taylor, Mid-Surrey	74	78	74	83	309
H.B. Simpson, St Annes Old	77	80	78	75	310

Abe Mitchell, Sonning	76	78	79	79	312
Tom Williamson, Notts	75	79	79	79	312
R.G. Wilson, Croham Hurst	76	77	80	80	313

1920 DEAL

George Duncan, Hanger Hill	80	80	71	72	303
Sandy Herd, Coombe Hill	72	81	77	75	305
Ted Ray, Oxhey	72	83	78	73	306
Abe Mitchell, North Foreland	74	73	84	76	307
Len Holland, Northampton	80	78	71	79	308
Jim Barnes, USA	79	74	77	79	309

1921 ST ANDREWS

Jock Hutchison, USA	72	75	79	70	296
*Roger Wethered, Royal and Ancient	78	75	72	71	296
(Hutchison won play-off 150 to 159)					
T. Kerrigan, USA	74	80	72	72	298
Arthur G. Havers, West Lancs	76	74	77	72	299
George Duncan, Hanger Hill	74	75	78	74	301

1922 SANDWICH

Walter Hagen, USA	76	73	79	72	300
George Duncan, Hangar Hill	76	75	81	69	301
Jim Barnes, USA	75	76	77	73	301
Jock Hutchison, USA	79	74	73	76	302
Charles Whitcombe, Dorchester	77	79	72	75	303
J.H. Taylor, Mid-Surrey	73	78	76	77	304

1923 TROON

Arthur G. Havers, Coombe Hill	73	73	73	76	295
Walter Hagen, USA	76	71	74	75	296
Macdonald Smith, USA	80	73	69	75	297
Joe Kirkwood, Australia	72	79	69	78	298
Tom Fernie, Turnberry	73	78	74	75	300
George Duncan, Hanger Hill	79	75	74	74	302
Charles A. Whitcombe, Landsdowne	70	76	74	82	302

1924 HOYLAKE

Walter Hagen, USA	77	73	74	77	301
Ernest Whitcombe, Came Down	77	70	77	78	302
Macdonald Smith, USA	76	74	77	77	304
F. Ball, Langley Park	78	75	74	77	304
J.H. Taylor, Mid-Surrey	75	74	79	79	307
George Duncan, Hanger Hill	74	79	74	81	308
Aubrey Boomer, St Cloud, Paris	75	78	76	79	308

1925 PRESTWICK

Jim Barnes, USA	70	77	79	74	300
Archie Compston, North Manchester	76	75	75	75	301
Ted Ray, Oxhey	77	76	75	73	301
Macdonald Smith, USA	76	69	76	82	303
Abe Mitchell, Unattached	77	76	75	77	305

1926 ROYAL LYTHAM

*Robert T. Jones Jr, USA	72	72	73	74	291
Al Watrous, USA	71	75	69	78	293

Walter Hagen, USA	68	77	74	76	295
George von Elm, USA	75	72	76	72	295
Abe Mitchell, Unattached	78	78	72	71	299
T. Barber, Cavendish	77	73	78	71	299

1927 ST ANDREWS

*Robert T. Jones Jr, USA	68	72	73	72	285
Aubrey Boomer, St Cloud, Paris	76	70	73	72	291
Fred Robson, Cooden Beach	76	72	69	74	291
Joe Kirkwood, Australia	72	72	75	74	293
Ernest Whitcombe, Bournemouth	74	73	73	73	293
Charles Whitcombe, Crews Hill	74	76	71	75	296

1928 SANDWICH

Walter Hagen, USA	75	73	72	72	292
Gene Sarazen, USA	72	76	73	73	294
Archie Compston, Unattached	75	74	73	73	295
Percy Alliss, Berlin	75	76	75	72	298
Fred Robson, Cooden Beach	79	73	73	73	298
Jose Jurado, Argentina	74	71	76	80	301
Aubrey Boomer, St Cloud, Paris	79	73	77	72	301
Jim Barnes, USA	81	73	76	71	301

1929 MUIRFIELD

Walter Hagen, USA	75	67	75	75	292
John Farrell, USA	72	75	76	75	298
Leo Diegel, USA	71	69	82	77	299
Abe Mitchell, St Albans	72	72	78	78	300
Percy Alliss, Berlin	69	76	76	79	300
Bobby Cruickshank, USA	73	74	78	76	301

1930 HOYLAKE

*Robert T. Jones Jr, USA	70	72	74	75	291
Leo Diegel, USA	74	73	71	75	293
Macdonald Smith, USA	70	77	75	71	293
Fred Robson, Cooden Beach	71	72	78	75	296
Horton Smith, USA	72	73	78	73	296
Archie Compston, Coombe Hill	74	73	68	82	297
Jim Barnes, USA	71	77	72	77	297

1931 CARNOUSTIE

Tommy Armour, USA	73	75	77	71	296
Jose Jurado, Argentina	76	71	73	77	297
Percy Alliss, Berlin	74	78	73	73	298
Gene Sarazen, USA	74	76	75	73	298
Macdonald Smith, USA	75	77	71	76	299
John Farrell, USA	72	77	75	75	299

1932 PRINCE'S

Gene Sarazen, USA	70	69	70	74	283
Macdonald Smith, USA	71	76	71	70	288
Arthur G. Havers, Sandy Lodge	74	71	68	76	289
Charles Whitcombe, Crews Hill	71	73	73	75	292
Percy Alliss, Beaconsfield	71	71	78	72	292
Alf Padgham, Royal Ashdown Forest	76	72	74	70	292

1933 ST ANDREWS

Densmore Shute, USA	73	73	73	73	292
Craig Wood, USA	77	72	68	75	292
(Shute won play-off 149 to 154)					
Sid Easterbrook, Knowle	73	72	71	77	293
Gene Sarazen, USA	72	73	73	75	293
Leo Diegel, USA	75	70	71	77	293
Olin Dutra, USA	76	76	70	72	294

1934 SANDWICH

Henry Cotton, Waterloo, Belgium	67	65	72	79	283
Sid Brews, South Africa	76	71	70	71	288
Alf Padgham, Sundridge Park	71	70	75	74	290
Macdonald Smith, USA	77	71	72	72	292
Joe Kirkwood, USA	74	69	71	78	292
Marcel Dallemagne, France	71	73	71	77	292

1935 MUIRFIELD

Alf Perry, Leatherhead	69	75	67	72	283
Alf Padgham, Sundridge Park	70	72	74	71	287
Charles Whitcombe, Crews Hill	71	68	73	76	288
Bert Gadd, Brand Hall	72	75	71	71	289
Lawson Little, USA	75	71	74	69	289
Henry Picard, USA	72	73	72	75	292

1936 HOYLAKE

Alf Padgham, Sundridge Park	73	72	71	71	287
Jimmy Adams, Romford	71	73	71	73	288
Henry Cotton, Waterloo, Belgium	73	72	70	74	289
Marcel Dallemagne, France	73	72	75	69	289
Percy Alliss, Leeds Municipal	74	72	74	71	291
T. Green, Burnham Beeches	74	72	70	75	291
Gene Sarazen, USA	73	75	70	73	291

1937 CARNOUSTIE

Henry Cotton, Ashridge	74	72	73	71	290
Reg Whitcombe, Parkstone	72	70	74	76	292
Charles Lacey, USA	76	75	70	72	293
Charles Whitcombe, Crews Hill	73	71	74	76	294
Bryon Nelson, USA	75	76	71	74	296
Ed Dudley, USA	70	74	78	75	297

1938 SANDWICH

Reg Whitcombe, Parkstone	71	71	75	78	295
Jimmy Adams, Royal Liverpool	70	71	78	78	297
Henry Cotton, Ashridge	74	73	77	74	298
Alf Padgham, Sundridge Park	74	72	75	82	303
Jack Busson, Pannal	71	69	83	80	303
Richard Burton, Sale	71	69	78	85	303
Allan Dailey, Wanstead	73	72	80	78	303

1939 ST ANDREWS

Richard Burton, Sale	70	72	77	71	290
Johnny Bulla, USA	77	71	71	73	292
Johnny Fallon, Huddersfield	71	73	71	79	294
Bill Shankland, Temple Newsam	72	73	72	77	294
Alf Perry, Leatherhead	71	74	73	76	294

Reg Whitcombe, Parkstone	71	75	74	74	294
Sam King, Knole Park	74	72	75	73	294

1946 ST ANDREWS

Sam Snead, USA	71	70	74	75	290
Bobby Locke, South Africa	69	74	75	76	294
Johnny Bulla, USA	71	72	72	79	294
Charlie Ward, Little Aston	73	73	73	76	295
Henry Cotton, Royal Mid-Surrey	70	70	76	79	295
Dai Rees, Hindhead	75	67	73	80	295
Norman von Nida, Australia	70	76	74	75	295

1947 HOYLAKE

Fred Daly, Balmoral, Belfast	73	70	78	72	293
Reg Horne, Hendon	77	74	72	71	294
*Frank Stranahan, USA	71	79	72	72	294
Bill Shankland, Temple Newsam	76	74	75	70	295
Richard Burton, Coombe Hill	77	71	77	71	296
Charlie Ward, Little Aston	76	73	76	72	297
Sam King, Wildernesse	75	72	77	73	297
Arthur Lees, Dore and Totley	75	74	72	76	297
Johnny Bulla, USA	80	72	74	71	297
Henry Cotton, Royal Mid-Surrey	69	78	74	76	297
Norman von Nida, Australia	74	76	71	76	297

1948 MUIRFIELD

Henry Cotton, Royal Mid-Surrey	71	66	75	72	284
Fred Daly, Balmoral, Belfast	72	71	73	73	289
Norman von Nida, Australia	71	72	76	71	290
Roberto de Vicenzo, Argentina	70	73	72	75	290
Jack Hargreaves, Sutton Coldfield	76	68	73	73	290
Charlie Ward, Little Aston	69	72	75	74	290

1949 SANDWICH

Bobby Locke, South Africa	69	76	68	70	283
Harry Bradshaw, Kilcroney, Eire	68	77	68	70	283
(Locke won play-off 135 to 147)					
Roberto de Vicenzo, Argentina	68	75	73	69	285
Sam King, Knole Park	71	69	74	72	286
Charlie Ward, Little Aston	73	71	70	72	286
Arthur Lees, Dore and Totley	74	70	72	71	287
Max Faulkner, Royal Mid-Surrey	71	71	71	74	287

1950 TROON

Bobby Locke, South Africa	69	72	70	68	279
Roberto de Vicenzo, Argentina	72	71	68	70	281
Fred Daly, Balmoral, Belfast	75	72	69	66	282
Dai Rees, South Herts	71	68	72	71	282
E. Moore, South Africa	74	68	73	68	283
Max Faulkner, Royal Mid-Surrey	73	70	70	71	283

1951 ROYAL PORTRUSH

Max Faulkner, Unattached	71	70	70	74	285
Tony Cerda, Argentina	74	72	71	70	287
Charlie Ward, Little Aston	75	73	74	68	290
Fred Daly, Balmoral, Belfast	74	70	75	73	292
Jimmy Adams, Wentworth	68	77	75	72	292
Bobby Locke, South Africa	71	74	74	74	293

Bill Shankland, Temple Newsam	73	76	72	72	293
Norman Sutton, Leigh	73	70	74	76	293
Harry Weetman, Croham Hurst	73	71	75	74	293
Peter Thomson, Australia	70	75	73	75	293

1952 ROYAL LYTHAM

Bobby Locke, South Africa	69	71	74	73	287
Peter Thomson, Australia	68	73	77	70	288
Fred Daly, Balmoral, Belfast	67	69	77	76	289
Henry Cotton, Royal Mid-Surrey	75	74	74	71	294
Tony Cerda, Argentina	73	73	76	73	295
Sam King, Knole Park	71	74	74	76	295

1953 CARNOUSTIE

Ben Hogan, USA	73	71	70	68	282
*Frank Stranahan, USA	70	74	73	69	286
Dai Rees, South Herts	72	70	73	71	286
Peter Thomson, Australia	72	72	71	71	286
Tony Cerda, Argentina	75	71	69	71	286
Roberto de Vicenzo, Argentina	72	71	71	73	287

1954 ROYAL BIRKDALE

Peter Thomson, Australia	72	71	69	71	283
Sid Scott, Carlisle City	76	67	69	72	284
Dai Rees, South Herts	72	71	69	72	284
Bobby Locke, South Africa	74	71	69	70	284
Jimmy Adams, Royal Mid-Surrey	73	75	69	69	286
Tony Cerda, Argentina	71	71	73	71	286
J. Turnesa, USA	72	72	71	71	286

1955 ST ANDREWS

Peter Thomson, Australia	71	68	70	72	281
Johnny Fallon, Huddersfield	73	67	73	70	283
Frank Jowle, Edgbaston	70	71	69	74	284
Bobby Locke, South Africa	74	69	70	72	285
Tony Cerda, Argentina	73	71	71	71	286
Ken Bousfield, Coombe Hill	71	75	70	70	286
Harry Weetman, Croham Hurst	71	71	70	74	286
Bernard Hunt, Hartsbourne	70	71	74	71	286
Flory van Donck, Belgium	71	72	71	72	286

1956 HOYLAKE

Peter Thomson, Australia	70	70	72	74	286
Flory van Donck, Belgium	71	74	70	74	289
Roberto de Vicenzo, Argentina	71	70	79	70	290
Gary Player, South Africa	71	76	73	71	291
John Panton, Glenbervie	74	76	72	70	292
Henry Cotton, Temple	72	76	71	74	293
E. Bertolino, Argentina	69	72	76	76	293

1957 ST ANDREWS

Bobby Locke, South Africa	69	72	68	70	279
Peter Thomson, Australia	73	69	70	70	282
Eric Brown, Buchanan Castle	67	72	73	71	283
Angel Miguel, Spain	72	72	69	72	285
David Thomas, Sudbury	72	74	70	70	286
Tom Haliburton, Wentworth	72	73	68	73	286
*Dick Smith, Prestwick	71	72	72	71	286
Flory van Donck, Belgium	72	68	74	72	286

1958 ROYAL LYTHAM

Peter Thomson, Australia	66	72	67	73	278
David Thomson, Sudbury	70	68	69	71	278
(Thomson won play-off 139 to 143)					
Eric Brown, Buchanan Castle	73	70	65	71	279
Christy O'Connor, Killarney	67	68	73	71	279
Flory van Donck, Belgium	70	70	67	74	281
Leopoldo Ruiz, Argentina	71	65	72	73	281

1959 MUIRFIELD

Gary Player, South Africa	75	71	70	68	284
Flory van Donck, Belgium	70	70	73	73	286
Fred Bullock, Prestwick St Ninians	68	70	74	74	286
Sid Scott, Roehampton	73	70	73	71	287
Christy O'Connor, Royal Dublin	73	74	72	69	288
*Reid Jack, Dullatur	71	75	68	74	288
Sam King, Knole Park	70	74	68	76	288
John Panton, Glenbervie	72	72	71	73	288

1960 ST ANDREWS

Kel Nagle, Australia	69	67	71	71	278
Arnold Palmer, USA	70	71	70	68	279
Bernard Hunt, Hartsbourne	72	73	71	66	282
Harold Henning, South Africa	72	72	69	69	282
Roberto de Vicenzo, Argentina	67	67	75	73	282
*Guy Wolstenholme, Sunningdale	74	70	71	68	283

1961 ROYAL BIRKDALE

Arnold Palmer, USA	70	73	69	72	284
Dai Rees, South Herts	68	74	71	72	285
Christy O'Connor, Royal Dublin	71	77	67	73	288
Neil Coles, Coombe Hill	70	77	69	72	288
Eric Brown, Unattached	73	76	70	70	289
Kel Nagle, Australia	68	75	75	71	289

1962 TROON

Arnold Palmer, USA	71	69	67	69	276
Kel Nagle, Australia	71	71	70	70	282
Brian Huggett, Romford	75	71	74	69	289
Phil Rodgers, USA	75	70	72	72	289
Bob Charles, NZ	75	70	70	75	290
Sam Snead, USA	76	73	72	71	292
Peter Thomson, Australia	70	77	75	70	292

1963 ROYAL LYTHAM

Bob Charles, NZ	68	72	66	71	277
Phil Rodgers, USA	67	68	73	69	277
(Charles won play-off 140 to 148)					
Jack Nicklaus, USA	71	67	70	70	278
Kel Nagle, Australia	69	70	73	71	283
Peter Thomson, Australia	67	69	71	78	285
Christy O'Connor, Royal Dublin	74	68	76	68	286

1964 ST ANDREWS

Tony Lema, USA	73	68	68	70	279
Jack Nicklaus, USA	76	74	66	68	284
Roberto de Vicenzo, Argentina	76	72	70	67	285

Bernard Hunt, Hartsbourne	73	74	70	70	287
Bruce Devlin, Australia	72	72	73	73	290
Christy O'Connor, Royal Dublin	71	73	74	73	291
Harry Weetman, Selsdon Park	72	71	75	73	291

1965 ROYAL BIRKDALE

Peter Thomson, Australia	74	68	72	71	285
Christy O'Connor, Royal Dublin	69	73	74	71	287
Brian Huggett, Romford	73	68	76	70	287
Roberto de Vicenzo, Argentina	74	69	73	72	288
Kel Nagle, Australia	74	70	73	72	289
Tony Lema, USA	68	72	75	74	289
Bernard Hunt, Hartsbourne	74	74	70	71	289

1966 MUIRFIELD

Jack Nicklaus, USA	70	67	75	70	282
David Thomas, Dunham Forest	72	73	69	69	283
Doug Sanders, USA	71	70	72	70	283
Gary Player, South Africa	72	74	71	69	286
Bruce Devlin, Australia	73	69	74	70	286
Kel Nagle, Australia	72	68	76	70	286
Phil Rodgers, USA	74	66	70	76	286

1967 HOYLAKE

Roberto de Vicenzo, Argentina	70	71	67	70	278
Jack Nicklaus, USA	71	69	71	69	280
Clive Clark, Sunningdale	70	73	69	72	284
Gary Player, South Africa	72	71	67	74	284
Tony Jacklin, Potters Bar	73	69	73	70	285
Sebastian Miguel, Spain	72	74	68	72	286
Harold Henning, South Africa	74	70	71	71	286

1968 CARNOUSTIE

Gary Player, South Africa	74	71	71	73	289
Jack Nicklaus, USA	76	69	73	73	291
Bob Charles, NZ	72	72	71	76	291
Billy Casper, USA	72	68	74	78	292
Maurice Bembridge, Little Aston	71	75	73	74	293
Brian Barnes, Burnham & Berrow	70	74	80	71	295
Neil Coles, Coombe Hill	75	76	71	73	295
Gay Brewer, USA	74	73	72	76	295

1969 ROYAL LYTHAM

Tony Jacklin, Potters Bar	68	70	70	72	280
Bob Charles, NZ	66	69	75	72	282
Peter Thomson, Australia	71	70	70	72	283
Roberto de Vicenzo, Argentina	72	73	66	72	283
Christy O'Connor, Royal Dublin	71	65	74	74	284
Jack Nicklaus, USA	75	70	68	72	285
Davis Love Jr, USA	70	73	71	71	285

1970 ST ANDREWS

Jack Nicklaus, USA	68	69	73	73	283
Doug Sanders, USA	68	71	71	73	283
(Nicklaus won play-off 72 to 73)					
Harold Henning, South Africa	67	72	73	73	285
Lee Trevino, USA	68	68	72	77	285
Tony Jacklin, Potters Bar	67	70	73	76	286
Neil Coles, Coombe Hill	65	74	72	76	287

Peter Oosterhuis, Dulwich and Sydenham	73	69	69	76	287

1971 ROYAL BIRKDALE

Lee Trevino, USA	69	70	69	70	278
Lu Liang Huan, Taiwan	70	70	69	70	279
Tony Jacklin, Potters Bar	69	70	70	71	280
Craig de Foy, Coombe Hill	72	72	68	69	281
Jack Nicklaus, USA	71	71	72	69	283
Charles Coody, USA	74	71	70	68	283

1972 MUIRFIELD

Lee Trevino, USA	71	70	66	71	278
Jack Nicklaus, USA	70	72	71	66	279
Tony Jacklin, Potters Bar	69	72	67	72	280
Doug Sanders, USA	71	71	69	70	281
Brian Barnes, Fairway DR	71	72	69	71	283
Gary Player, South Africa	71	71	76	67	285

1973 TROON

Tom Weiskopf, USA	68	67	71	70	276
Neil Coles, Holiday Inns	71	72	70	66	279
Johnny Miller, USA	70	68	69	72	279
Jack Nicklaus, USA	69	70	76	65	280
Bert Yancey, USA	69	69	73	70	281
Peter Butler, Golf Domes	71	72	74	69	286

1974 ROYAL LYTHAM

Gary Player, South Africa	69	68	75	70	282
Peter Oosterhuis, Pacific Harbour	71	71	73	71	286
Jack Nicklaus, USA	74	72	70	71	287
Hubert Green, USA	71	74	72	71	288
Danny Edwards, USA	70	73	76	73	292
Lu Liang Huan, Taiwan	72	72	75	73	292

1975 CARNOUSTIE

Tom Watson, USA	71	67	69	72	279
Jack Newton, Australia	69	71	65	74	279
(Watson won play-off 71 to 72)					
Bobby Cole, South Africa	72	66	66	76	280
Jack Nicklaus, USA	69	71	68	72	280
Johnny Miller, USA	71	69	66	74	280
Graham Marsh, Australia	72	67	71	71	281

1976 ROYAL BIRKDALE

Johnny Miller, USA	72	68	73	66	279
Jack Nicklaus, USA	74	70	72	69	285
Severiano Ballesteros, Spain	69	69	73	74	285
Raymond Floyd, USA	76	67	73	70	286
Mark James, Burghley Park	76	72	74	66	288
Hubert Green, USA	72	70	78	68	288
Christy O'Connor Jr, Shannon	69	73	75	71	288
Tom Kite, USA	70	74	73	71	288
Tommy Horton, Royal Jersey	74	69	72	73	288

1977 TURNBERRY

Tom Watson, USA	68	70	65	65	268
Jack Nicklaus, USA	68	70	65	66	269

Hubert Green, USA	72	66	74	67	279
Lee Trevino, USA	68	70	72	70	280
Ben Crenshaw, USA	71	69	66	75	281
George Burns, USA	70	70	72	69	281

1978 ST ANDREWS

Jack Nicklaus, USA	71	72	69	69	281
Simon Owen, NZ	70	75	67	71	283
Ben Crenshaw, USA	70	69	73	71	283
Raymond Floyd, USA	69	75	71	68	283
Tom Kite, USA	72	69	72	70	283
Peter Oosterhuis, GB	72	70	69	73	284

1979 ROYAL LYTHAM

Severiano Ballesteros, Spain	73	65	75	70	283
Jack Nicklaus, USA	72	69	73	72	286
Ben Crenshaw, USA	72	71	72	71	286
Mark James, Burghley Park	76	69	69	73	287
Rodger Davis, Australia	75	70	70	73	288
Hale Irwin, USA	68	68	75	78	289

1980 MUIRFIELD

Tom Watson, USA	68	70	64	69	271
Lee Trevino, USA	68	67	71	69	275
Ben Crenshaw, USA	70	70	68	69	277
Jack Nicklaus, USA	73	67	71	69	280
Carl Mason, Unattached	72	69	70	69	280

1981 SANDWICH

Bill Rogers, USA	72	66	67	71	276
Bernhard Langer, Germany	73	67	70	70	280
Mark James, Otley	72	70	68	73	283
Raymond Floyd, USA	74	70	69	70	283
Sam Torrance, Caledonian Hotel	72	69	73	70	284
Bruce Leitzke, USA	76	69	71	69	285
Manuel Pinero, Spain	73	74	68	70	285

1982 TROON

Tom Watson, USA	69	71	74	70	284
Peter Oosterhuis, GB	74	67	74	70	285
Nick Price, South Africa	69	69	74	73	285
Nick Faldo, Glynwed Ltd	73	73	71	69	286
Des Smyth, EAL Tubes	70	69	74	73	286
Tom Purtzer, USA	76	66	75	69	286
Massy Kuramoto, Japan	71	73	71	71	286

1983 ROYAL BIRKDALE

Tom Watson, USA	67	68	70	70	275
Hale Irwin, USA	69	68	72	67	276
Andy Bean, USA	70	69	70	67	276
Graham Marsh, Australia	69	70	74	64	277
Lee Trevino, USA	69	66	73	70	278
Severiano Ballesteros, Spain	71	71	69	68	279
Harold Henning, South Africa	71	69	70	69	279

1984 ST ANDREWS

Severiano Ballesteros, Spain	69	68	70	69	276
Bernhard Langer, Germany	71	68	68	71	278
Tom Watson, USA	71	68	66	73	278

Fred Couples, USA	70	69	74	68	281
Lanny Wadkins, USA	70	69	73	69	281
Greg Norman, Australia	67	74	74	67	282
Nick Faldo, Glynwed Int.	69	68	76	69	282

1985 SANDWICH

Sandy Lyle, Scotland	68	71	73	70	282
Payne Stewart, USA	70	75	70	68	283
Jose Rivero, Spain	74	72	70	68	284
Christy O'Connor Jr, Ireland	64	76	72	72	284
Mark O'Meara, USA	70	72	70	72	284
David Graham, Australia	68	71	70	75	284
Bernhard Langer, Germany	72	69	68	75	284

1986 TURNBERRY

Greg Norman, Australia	74	63	74	69	280
Gordon J. Brand, England	71	68	75	71	285
Bernhard Langer, Germany	72	70	76	68	286
Ian Woosnam, Wales	70	74	70	72	286
Nick Faldo, England	71	70	76	70	287

1987 MUIRFIELD

Nick Faldo, England	68	69	71	71	279
Rodger Davis, Australia	64	73	74	69	280
Paul Azinger, USA	68	68	71	73	280
Ben Crenshaw, USA	73	68	72	68	281
Payne Stewart, USA	71	66	72	72	281
David Frost, South Africa	70	68	70	74	282
Tom Watson, USA	69	69	71	74	283

1988 ROYAL LYTHAM

Severiano Ballesteros, Spain	67	71	70	65	273
Nick Price, Zimbabwe	70	67	69	69	275
Nick Faldo, England	71	69	68	71	279
Fred Couples, USA	73	69	71	68	281
Gary Koch, USA	71	72	70	68	281
Peter Senior, Australia	70	73	70	69	282

1989 ROYAL TROON

Mark Calcavecchia, USA	71	68	68	68	275
Greg Norman, Australia	69	70	72	64	275
Wayne Grady, Australia	68	67	69	71	275
(Calcavecchia won four-hole play-off)					
Tom Watson, USA	69	68	68	72	277
Jodie Mudd, USA	73	67	68	70	278

FINAL RESULTS

HOLE		1	2	3	4	5	6	7	8	9	10	11	12	13	14	15	16	17	18	TOTAL
PAR		4	4	4	4	5	4	4	3	4	4	3	4	4	5	4	4	4	4	
Nick Faldo	Round 1	4	4	4	4	4	4	4	3	4	3	3	3	3	5	4	4	5	2	67
	Round 2	4	3	4	4	4	3	3	3	4	3	3	4	4	5	3	3	4	4	65
	Round 3	3	4	4	4	4	4	4	3	3	4	2	4	4	5	4	3	5	3	67
	Round 4	3	4	4	5	4	4	4	3	4	4	3	4	4	5	3	4	5	4	71-270
Mark McNulty	Round 1	3	4	4	5	4	4	4	3	4	4	3	4	4	7	4	4	5	4	74
	Round 2	4	3	4	4	5	4	5	3	3	3	2	4	4	5	3	4	4	4	68
	Round 3	3	3	4	5	4	3	3	3	3	4	3	4	4	5	4	5	4	4	68
	Round 4	3	4	3	4	5	4	3	3	4	3	3	3	4	4	3	4	4	4	65-275
Payne Stewart	Round 1	4	4	3	4	5	4	4	3	3	4	3	3	4	5	4	3	5	3	68
	Round 2	3	4	4	4	4	3	4	3	4	4	2	5	4	4	4	4	4	4	68
	Round 3	4	3	4	4	4	3	4	3	4	4	3	4	4	5	4	4	4	3	68
	Round 4	4	4	4	4	4	3	4	4	3	4	3	3	5	5	4	4	5	5	71-275
Jodie Mudd	Round 1	4	4	4	4	4	4	4	3	4	4	3	4	4	5	4	4	5	4	72
	Round 2	3	3	4	4	4	4	4	2	3	4	3	3	4	4	4	5	5	3	66
	Round 3	4	4	4	4	4	4	5	3	4	4	3	3	5	4	4	4	5	4	72
	Round 4	3	4	4	5	5	4	3	2	4	3	2	3	4	4	3	4	6	3	66-276
Ian Woosnam	Round 1	4	4	4	3	5	3	5	3	3	4	3	3	4	5	4	3	4	4	68
	Round 2	4	3	3	4	5	3	3	3	4	3	2	4	4	5	5	4	6	4	69
	Round 3	3	4	3	4	5	4	3	2	4	5	3	4	4	5	4	4	5	4	70
	Round 4	3	5	4	4	4	4	3	3	3	3	2	4	4	6	4	4	5	4	69-276
Greg Norman	Round 1	3	4	4	4	4	4	4	3	4	3	3	3	4	4	4	4	4	3	66
	Round 2	4	5	4	3	5	4	3	2	3	3	3	4	5	3	4	3	4	4	66
	Round 3	4	5	4	3	5	3	4	3	5	4	3	5	5	5	5	5	4	4	76
	Round 4	4	4	5	4	5	4	3	3	4	3	3	4	4	4	3	4	5	3	69-277
Ian Baker-Finch	Round 1	3	5	4	4	4	4	4	2	3	3	3	4	4	5	4	4	5	3	68
	Round 2	4	4	4	4	4	4	5	2	4	4	3	4	5	5	4	4	4	4	72
	Round 3	3	3	4	3	3	3	4	2	4	3	3	3	4	5	4	4	5	4	64
	Round 4	4	3	4	5	4	4	4	3	4	4	3	4	5	4	5	5	5	4	73-277
David Graham	Round 1	5	4	4	5	4	5	3	3	4	4	4	3	4	5	3	4	4	4	72
	Round 2	4	4	4	5	5	4	4	2	5	3	3	4	5	5	4	4	3	3	71
	Round 3	4	5	4	5	5	4	3	3	4	3	3	4	4	4	3	4	4	4	70
	Round 4	3	3	4	4	4	4	4	3	4	3	3	4	4	5	3	4	3	4	66-279
Steve Pate	Round 1	4	4	3	4	4	3	5	3	4	4	3	4	4	5	4	4	4	4	70
	Round 2	4	4	5	3	5	4	3	3	3	3	3	3	4	5	4	5	3	4	68
	Round 3	3	4	4	4	5	4	4	2	4	4	3	4	5	5	4	4	5	4	72
	Round 4	4	5	4	4	4	4	3	2	3	3	3	4	4	5	4	4	5	4	69-279
Donnie Hammond	Round 1	5	3	3	4	5	3	4	4	4	4	4	3	4	5	4	4	5	3	70
	Round 2	4	4	4	6	4	4	3	3	3	3	3	4	4	4	4	5	5	4	71
	Round 3	4	3	4	5	4	4	3	3	3	3	3	4	4	6	3	4	5	3	68
	Round 4	3	4	4	4	3	4	4	4	4	3	3	4	5	5	3	4	5	4	70-279
Corey Pavin	Round 1	4	4	3	4	5	4	4	4	4	4	3	5	4	4	3	3	5	4	71
	Round 2	4	4	4	4	5	3	4	3	4	3	3	4	4	5	4	4	4	3	69
	Round 3	3	4	4	4	5	4	3	3	4	4	3	3	4	5	4	4	4	3	68
	Round 4	3	3	4	4	5	3	4	3	4	4	4	4	3	5	4	6	4	4	71-279

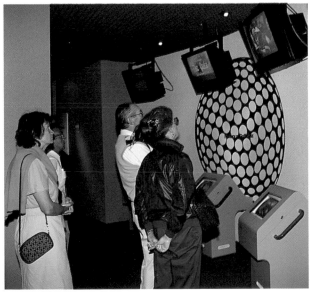

The new British Golf Museum was completed in time for the Open Championship. The Museum is located just behind the R&A Clubhouse.